THE GREEK ISLANDS
Genius Loci

View of Naxos island seen through the monumental doorway of the Archaic temple.
Thomas Hope (1769-1831)   Watercolour, 44 x 29 cm.   Benaki Museum, Inv. No. 27375.
© 2010 Benaki Museum, Athens.

Author's acknowledgements

This series of twenty books covering the Aegean Islands is the fruit of many years of solitary dedication to a job difficult to accomplish given the extent of the subject matter and the geography involved. My belief throughout has been that only what is seen with the eyes can trustfully be written about; and to that end I have attempted to walk, ride, drive, climb, sail and swim these Islands in order to inspect everything talked about here. There will be errors in this text inevitably for which, although working in good faith, I alone am responsible. Notwithstanding, I am confident that these are the best, most clearly explanatory and most comprehensive artistic accounts currently available of this vibrant and historically dense corner of the Mediterranean.

Professor Robin Barber, author of the last, general, *Blue Guide to Greece* (based in turn on Stuart Rossiter's masterful text of the 1960s), has been very generous with support and help; and I am also particularly indebted to Charles Arnold for meticulously researched factual data on the Islands and for his support throughout this project. I could not have asked for a more saintly and helpful editor, corrector and indexer than Judy Tither. Efi Stathopoulou, Peter Cocconi, Marc René de Montalembert, Valentina Ivancich, William Forrester and Geoffrey Cox have all given invaluable help; and I owe a large debt of gratitude to John and Jay Rendall for serial hospitality and encouragement. For companionship on many journeys, I would like to thank a number of dear friends: Graziella Seferiades, Ivan Tabares, Matthew Kidd, Martin Leon, my group of Louisianan friends, and my brother Iain— all of whose different reactions to and passions for Greece have been a constant inspiration.

This work is dedicated with admiration and deep affection to Ivan de Jesus Tabares-Valencia who, though a native of the distant Andes mountains, from the start understood the profound spiritual appeal of the Aegean world.

McGILCHRIST'S GREEK ISLANDS

9 EUBOEA

GENIUS LOCI PUBLICATIONS
London

McGilchrist's Greek Islands 9 Euboea
First edition

Published by Genius Loci Publications
54 Eccleston Road, London W13 0RL

Nigel McGilchrist © 2010
Nigel McGilchrist has asserted his moral rights.

ISBN 978-1-907859-15-1

A CIP catalogue record of this book is available from the British Library.

The author and publisher cannot accept responsibility or liability for
information contained herein, this being in some cases difficult to verify
and subject to change.

Layout and copy-editing by Judy Tither

Cover design by Kate Buckle

Maps and plans by Nick Hill Design

Printed and bound in Great Britain by TJ International Ltd, Padstow, Cornwall

The island maps in this series are based on the cartography of
Terrain Maps
Karneadou 4, 106 75 Athens, Greece
T: +30 210 609 5759, Fx: +30 210 609 5859
terrain@terrainmaps.gr
www.terrainmaps.gr

This book is one of twenty which comprise the complete, detailed
manuscript which the author prepared for the *Blue Guide: Greece,
the Aegean Islands* (2010), and on which the *Blue Guide* was
based. Some of this text therefore appears in the *Blue Guide*.

A NOTE ON THE TEXT & MAPS

Some items in the text are marked with an asterisk: these may be monuments, landscapes, curiosities or individual artefacts and works of art. The asterisk is not simply an indication of the renown of a particular place or item, but is intended to draw the reader's attention to things that have a uniquely interesting quality or are of particular beauty.

A small number of hotels and eateries are also marked with asterisks in the *Practical Information* sections, implying that their quality or their setting is notably special. These books do not set out to be guides to lodging and eating in the Islands, and our recommendations here are just an attempt to help with a few suggestions for places that have been selected with an eye to simplicity and unpretentiousness. We believe they may be the kind of places that a reader of this book would be seeking and would enjoy.

On the island maps:

⁂   denotes a site with visible prehistoric or ancient remains

✝   denotes a church referred to in the text
(on Island Maps only rural churches are marked)

✝   denotes a monastery, convent or large church referred to in the text

◫   denotes a Byzantine or Mediaeval castle

▌   denotes an ancient stone tower

♨   denotes an important fresh-water or geothermic spring

⛴   denotes a harbour with connecting ferry services

Road and path networks:

-     a continuous line denotes a metalled road or unsurfaced track feasible for motors

-     a dotted line denotes footpath only

CONTENTS

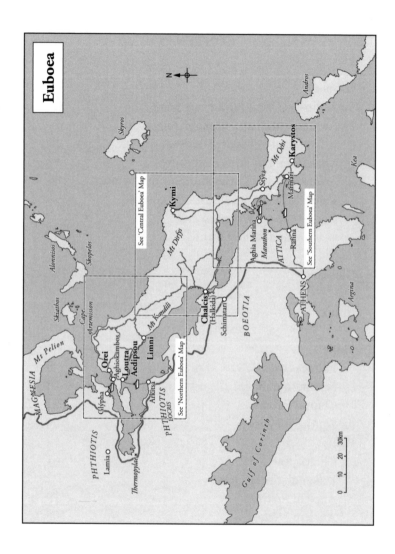

Euboea

EUBOEA
(EVVIA)

The grandeur and beauty of Euboea's landscapes are matched only by their constantly unfolding variety. The island is like a microcosm of all of Greece: the northern tip has the feel of the wooded and bucolic landscapes of Corfu; the mountainous gorges of the centre are like parts of Epirus and Roumeli; the valleys inland of Kymi have a gentleness and a wealth of painted churches which remind one of parts of the Peloponnese; the area around Dystos feels uncannily like Boeotia; and the south of the island, hemmed by windy beaches, is wild and rugged in the grandest Cycladic manner. On top of all this, there are parts of the island that are unlike anywhere else at all, such as the majestic, watered valleys of Dírfys and Ochi—the island's highest mountains, with their impressive and puzzling stone structures known as '*drakospita*', or 'dragon's houses', which are unique to Euboea. The mountains of Dirfys and Ochi and Kandili—all of them with summits equivalent to or substantially higher than Ben Nevis—are so fundamental to the appearance and the water and the weather of the island, that they merit individual exploration. Each possesses a strong personality, quite distinct from the other two.

Lying so close to the body of Greece, Euboea maintains much of the welcome normality of mainland life, yet it conserves the tranquillity and individuality of an island. There is no airport and the several harbours of access are small and informal. It is possible to drive to the island across the old or the new Euripus bridge. And once out of the busy capital of Chalcis, you can be in forests and gorges and mountains within a matter of minutes. Some of Greece's remotest villages even are to be found at the island's southeastern corner.

The long, winding ridge of the island is like a mountainous breakwater, protecting the eastern flank of Greece. In the placid stretch of safe water in its lee it has nurtured a number of rich, productive and very ancient centres which flourished in prehistoric and early historic times—*Eretria*, *Chalcis* and at Lefkandí. Fertile Euboea was sometimes called the 'larder of Greece': even the sound of its name '*Εὔ-βοια*' seemed to some to imply the quality of its livestock.[1] It later exported grain to Rome—together with the largest quantity of decorative marble from any single place in the Mediterranean. The Roman Imperial Fora

---

[1] Probably no more than a 'folk-etymology'. The root '-*βοια*' is more likely to be cognate with the name of '*Βοιω-τία*' which lies directly across the water, than with '*βόες*', meaning 'oxen'.

are everywhere built and lined with the blue-veined Karystos marble from Euboea—just as those who built those
same *fora*, may have been sustained by the island's grain.

Because of its geographical shape, Euboea requires
a meandering exploration up and down its protracted
length. This survey begins at the north and finishes in the
southeastern extremity of the island beside the wild Cavo
Doro straits, for no better reason than that we read a page
from top to bottom. But a journey for many will begin
at the island's capital, Chalcis, by the Euripus bridge: for
others, at Karystos in the south, at the nearest point to
Athens. For this reason, the description of the island has
been based on five different centres—Aedipsos, Limni,
Chalcis, Kymi and Karystos—from which it radiates out
into the surrounding areas of the island, so that the reader may approach the discovery of this richly rewarding
island in whichever order should suit best.

HISTORY

Running parallel to the eastern coast of mainland Greece for almost 180km—and often called '*Mákris*' in the Byzantine period because of its considerable length—Euboea all but encloses a large and tranquil inland water which favoured the development of important settlements in prehistoric and early historic times. The coastal plains to the northwest and southeast of Chalcis supported a scattering of Stone Age and Bronze Age communities, the best known and explored being the Early Helladic settlement on the small promontory of Mánika near Nea Artaki. In the Bronze Age, Euboea shared the culture of the Cyclades. The island has three distinct geographic zones, each supposed to have been originally settled by different groups of colonists from Thessaly: 'Ellopians' in the north, 'Abantes' in the centre and west, and 'Dryopes' in the south. It was only later, at the turn of the 1st millennium BC that Ionians from Attica, Aeolians from Phthiotis, and Dorians from the Peloponnese are said to have arrived. Although a number of cities emerged in later Antiquity at different points on Euboea, the north of the island was always dominated by the city of *Histiaia-Oreos*, the centre of the island by the rich and important cities of *Eretria* and *Chalcis*, and the south by *Karystos* and, to a lesser extent, *Geraistos*. Located between *Eretria* and *Chalcis* is Lefkandí—a highly significant site occupied from the Early to Late Helladic period and in the Geometric period. As well as yielding the largest building yet known to us from the 10th century BC in Greece, Lefkandí and its unusual finds have notably amplified our previously scant knowledge of the culture of its period. Through it we understand better the transition from the Mycenaean period into the so-called 'Dark Age' in Greece.

Both *Eretria* and *Chalcis* founded their own colonies on the coasts of Macedonia, Thrace, Italy and Sicily, as well as in the islands of the Aegean. They were also leading participants in the Greek *emporion* at Al Mina in Syria. At home they were in constant competition as rivals for the possession of the fertile Lelantine Plain which extended between them. On more than one occasion the contention erupted into armed conflict, and Herodotus and Thucydides imply that other Greek states were involved in this bitter and largely unresolved war. At the end of the 6th century BC, when *Chalcis* allied itself with Boeotia against Athens in a failed attempt to restore Hippias, the exiled tyrant of Athens, retribution was swift to follow: the Athenians crossed the Euripus strait in 506 BC, defeated the Chalcidians and divided their land up between 5,000 clerurchs (Herodotus, *Hist.* V, 77). *Eretria* suffered also, but at different hands, when the Persians attacked and burned the city in 490 BC and enslaved its inhabitants in retaliation for its support of the Ionian revolt. Although later rebuilt, *Eretria* never fully recovered her former power.

It was off the north coast of Euboea near Cape Artemision, that Greek ships boldly attempted to delay Xerxes's advance into Greece in July of 480 BC, and successfully separated his navy from his land forces for a short period. In the same campaign, a number of Persian ships were also lost in bad weather in the treacherous waters of the Kaphireas Strait, off the island's south coast. After the Persian wars, the whole of Euboea became subject to Athens and was a member of the Delian League. It was not long before this became a source of resentment and led to two concerted bids for freedom: first in 446 BC, when the island revolted but was re-conquered by Pericles and the inhabitants of *Histiaia-Oreos* were expelled and replaced by Athenian clerurchs; then with a second and more successful revolt in 411 BC, at a time when Athens was weakened by its disastrous venture in Sicily. In the same year the inhabitants of Chalcis, with the cooperation of Boeotia, built a bridge over the Euripus channel to hinder and control the maritime trade of Athens. In his *Peloponnesian War* (VIII. 96), Thucydides deemed Euboea of 'greater value to Athens than Attica itself'.

For a short period after 378 BC, the Athenians persuaded most of the Euboean cities to join their new maritime league. But with the ascendancy of Boeotian power in the wake of its defeat of Sparta at the battle of Leuctra in 371 BC, the island came under the control of Thebes. In 358 BC it was liberated by the Athenian general, Chares, who restored the island's alliance with Athens. Twenty years later, after the battle of Chaeronea in 338 BC, the island fell under Macedonian control. It was in this period that Aristotle fled from Athens to settle in Chalcis, and died after a brief sojourn in 322 BC.

The Romans first moved into Euboea in 199 BC, capturing first *Histiaia* and then *Eretria* the following year. By 196 BC the whole island had been taken from Macedonian control by the Roman general Titus Quinctius Flamininus, who declared it free. The two cities of *Aedipsos* and *Karystos* appear to have flourished in Imperial times, the latter principally on its favoured marble quarries; but Chalcis, though diminished in importance, remained the island's chief city.

Notices from Byzantine Euboea are sufficient only to show that Byzantium had to struggle to maintain control of the island. The city of Chalcis was still clearly a busy and productive enough port to attract the attention of the Saracen emir of Tarsus, who sailed across the Aegean at the end of the 9th century with the intention of sacking the town, but was defeated and killed by a detachment of Byzantine troops. In 1147 Roger II of Sicily appears to have used his army to kidnap the silk-workers of Chalcis; and the island's coasts were plundered not long after by the navy of William I 'The Bad', king of Sicily, fresh from a victory over the Byzantine forces of John Dukas in 1159. In the wake of the Fourth Crusade, the island had originally been taken by Jacques d'Avesnes in 1205. When he died without heirs, it was divided in 1209 into the three baronies (called 'triarchies') of Chalcis, Karystos and Oreos, which owed allegiance to the Frankish 'king of Salonica', Boniface of Monferrat. The baronies were subdivided latterly into smaller fiefdoms held by Frankish nobles who controlled small areas of the island from their fortified towers. The 14th century saw a concerted and increasing

Venetian domination of the ports of the island, and by 1366 the Venetians were effectively masters of almost the whole of Euboea. Their name for the island was '*Negroponte*', a fanciful variant of '*Egripo*'—itself a corruption of '*Euripo*' or '*Evripo*', the name of the channel separating the island from the mainland at Chalcis. Under the Venetians, Negroponte ranked as a kingdom, and its standard was one of the three hoisted in St Mark's Square—symbolic of the importance which the island had to Venice as a principal centre of influence and control in the Aegean area.

In July 1470 the Ottoman forces of Mehmet the Conqueror laid siege to Chalcis and, not without difficulty, wrested the city and control of the island from Venice. The island thenceforth came under the immediate rule of a *Kaptan Paşa*, or high admiral of the Ottoman Empire. After the War of Independence, Euboea passed to Greece in 1833. It was in this period that the prominent British Philhellene, Edward Noel, purchased the lands around Prokopi in Northern Euboea from a departing Ottoman official (*see p. 46*)—a policy originally promoted by the Government of Kapodistrias to encourage the management of rural areas and to prevent depopulation. In similar fashion, a certain number of Moslems, nearly all of whom were ethnic Albanians, were permitted by special decree to remain on the island. In practice much of the southern and central part of the island had historically received Albanian settlers, a policy initiated in the 15th century by the Venetians.

Although by the early 20th century Euboea had become a backwater supplying timber and building materials to Athens, the development of mining created employment and led to a measure of industrialisation. There was bitter resistance to the Axis Occupation, and strong support for the popular forces of ELAS (the *Ellinikos Laïkos Apeleftherotikos Stratos* or 'Greek People's Liberation Army') and the Democratic Army in the mountains during the Civil War period between 1944 and 1949. Northern Euboea was controlled by ELAS as early as June 1943. In the summer of 2007 the central southern area around Styra, and some areas further north, were devastated by forest fires.

The length of the island has been divided into six segments:
North Euboea
- *Aedipsos, Oreí, and the northeast of the island*
- *Around Limni and Prokopi: north central Euboea*

Central Euboea
- *Chalcis, Eretria and Amarynthos*
- *Around Mount Dírfys and Mount Olympos*
- *Kymi, and the central east of the island*

Southern Euboea
- *Lake Dystos to Karystos, and around Mount Ochi*

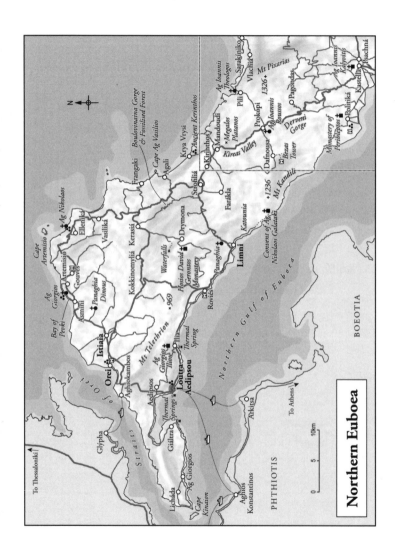

Northern Euboea

AEDIPSOS, OREI
& THE NORTH EAST

(Loutrá Aedipsoú = 0.0km for distances in this section)

(Car ferry connections to Loutrá Aedipsoú from Arkitsa on the mainland opposite, approximately every 30 mins from 7 am–9 pm in summer.)

With an attractive position and an air of passé gentility, **Loutrá Aedipsoú**, has something of the look and feel of a spa in the Italian Lakes. The verdant setting, the generally calm waters of the Euboean Gulf and the variety of stately 19th and early 20th century buildings (the *Herakleion, Stadion* and *Aigli* hotels, the public school, the neoclassical bath-house, etc.) make it a characterful and increasingly popular place to stay although much still needs to be spent to improve the fabric of the town. Ancient *Aedepsos* and its waters were popular with the Romans who were the first systematically to develop a thermal station here. Evidence of this can be seen in the hill, crowned by the church of Aghios Phanourios, directly behind the new Municipal Thermal Baths about 400m in from the south shore. The main springs originally rose in a grotto here, known as '**Sulla's Cave**'. The source was covered in a structure in Roman times: the cruciform design of its four vaults can still clearly be seen. Two **inscribed statue bases** lying at the entrance commemorate two patrons of the waters—the Emperors Hadrian and Septimius Severus.

THE THERMAL WATERS OF AEDIPSOS

The hot springs were a centre of cult from ancient times and were probably linked to the worship of Hercules. Aristotle noted them in his *Meteorologica* and Strabo referred to them as the 'Springs of Hercules'. The town grew up in the Hellenistic period and was visited by later Macedonian kings. One of the most famous visitors in the Roman period was Sulla, who came here to cure his gout; Plutarch describes the great banquets he gave. The spa achieved its greatest prosperity between 100 BC and 400 AD when numerous emperors and dignitaries visited, including Hadrian, Septimius Severus and Constantine the Great. The spa suffered with the arrival of Christianity when early Christians attacked what they saw as a cause of the dissipation of the inhabitants. It revived after the establishment of a bishopric in the 8th century, under the Metropolitan of Athens.

Under Frankish rule the town was known as 'Lipso'. It went into decline as a result of the growth of piracy and in the 15th century was laid waste by raiders. After Greek Independence little happened until the end of the 19th century when the spa was gradually developed under the influence of a new European predilection for 'taking waters'. It became the most fashionable resort in Greece for a time after World War I when the poet Cavafy was a visitor and well-to-do Athenians came to gamble in its Casino.

The water can be taken today (as guest or non-resident) in any one of the larger spa hotels, such as the *Avra Hotel* or the grander *Thermae Sylla* (Sulla), which was founded in 1896 and has received in its history such illustrious guests as Greta Garbo, Maria Callas and Winston Churchill. Otherwise there are the main Municipal Thermal Baths, now housed in a large ungainly building—a poor but more practical successor to the grand, neoclassical baths of yore. Most simply, the waters can be enjoyed on the main, south-facing beach where there are underwater hot springs in addition to the water which flows from the sources into the sea: the warmth and sulphur attract a unique diversity of fish and marine-life. The waters rise at temperatures between 34° and 71°C and enjoy a reputation for curing gout, rheumatism, sciatica and arthritis. The ancients believed, probably not erroneously, that the springs were in some way connected with those of Thermopylae on the opposite, mainland coast.

A small **Archaeological Collection** (*notionally open 10–1 daily, except Sun, July–Sept, but currently closed for lack of staff*) is gathered in two rooms on the upper floor of the Municipal Bathing Centre.

Room I exhibits prehistoric finds, including fragments of Mycenaean pottery and a **bronze sword** of the same epoch, found near Kastaniotissa; *Room II* has mostly inscriptions, and architectural and sculptural fragments in marble from the city's classical and Byzantine buildings, including areas of the 5th century **mosaic floor** from the *thermae*. Also exhibited in the upper floor of the hallway of the building, and freely accessible whenever the baths are open (*daily 7–9*), are two pieces of note: the headless, 1st century AD statue of a man wearing a *himation* (the missing head was originally part of the whole single piece of marble), and a fine **Roman relief, figuring the bow and pelt of Hercules,** in which there is a pleasing and harmonious play of contours and forms.

A number of pieces (inscribed, statue bases and other fragments) lie to either side of the entrance to the building and in the adjacent park.

Next door to the Municipal Baths building stands the former **neoclassical Bath House** with its horseshoe of private, marble bathing tubs, and a high central hall, currently in a perilous state of disrepair.

AROUND AEDIPSOS
LICHADA (WEST)

To the west of Loutrá Aedipsoú, pushing deep into the Malian Gulf, stretches the tranquil **Lichada peninsula**, dense with pines and olive groves which clad the headland's graceful summit of Xerosouvála (738m). The mountain and its offshore islets are associated in myth with the hapless servant, Lichas, who delivered the Shirt of Nessus to Hercules and was, for his service, hurled down into the sea here by the hero (Ovid, *Metamorphoses* IX, 211). The two largest settlements of **Giáltra** (14km), in the east, and **Licháda** (29km), towards the western point, both have old centres with pleasing stone houses and extensive views from their high positions. Giáltra has a harbour on the shore below with its own **therapeutic springs** by the sea—**Loutrá Giáltron**. The water is of milder temperature than at Aedipsos (39°–42°C); there are a series of bathing huts, beyond which the water flows out eventually onto the beach. From Licháda the road leads down to **Cape Kinaion** (33.5km)— a beautiful spot, popular for bathing, with the islets and the sweep of the Phthiotian and Thessalian shores in front. Little remains of the temple of Zeus *Kinaios* which stood to the north of here, other than an eroded piece of frieze lying beside the church of SS. Helen and Constantine which stands by the edge of the road back to Aghios Giorgios from the cape. There has been speculation as to the site near this cape of Ancient *Dios*, mentioned by Homer (*Iliad* II, 538) as having 'a steep citadel'.

ILIA (SOUTHEAST)

To the southeast of Loutrá Aedipsoú, the newly constructed road to Limni hugs the shore beneath the steep slopes of Mount Teléthrion (969m). At 9.5km is the small fishing village of **Ilia**—once accessible only by boat— spread along a protected beach with a number of attractive fish tavernas. At the eastern extremity of the beach an abundant **hot spring** (65°C) of highly ferrous water gushes from the rock and disperses in the sea, depositing an orange coloured mud of therapeutic qualities. This is another of the group of springs (Giáltra, Aedipsos, and Thermopylae on the opposite mainland shore) of common geological origin, ranged around the northern end of the gulf of Euboea. From Ilia, a track (*in poor condition*) leads 8km up the mountainside to the remote and dramatic site of the 18th century **monastery of Aghios Giorgios Iliou**, occupying possibly the same location as the oracle-sanctuary of Apollo *Selinuntios* which Strabo mentions. The *catholicon* is decorated with late Byzantine wall-paintings and a carved wooden iconostasis of 1834. Five kilometres beyond Ilia towards Limni is a sister convent of **Aghia Irini Chrysovalantou**; the position is also fine, but the fabric modern.

OREI AND ISTIAIA (NORTH)

The road north from Loutrá Aedipsoú reaches the north coast of the island at **Aghiókambos** (7.5km), where the small car ferry for Glyfa on the opposite mainland coast (16km from the Athens/Thessaloniki highway) runs every two hours from 7 am–9 pm, daily. Shortly beyond is the small port of **Oreí** (12km)—one of the most interesting towns in Northern Euboea.

The modern settlement occupies the site of Ancient *His-tiaea*—called '*polystaphylos*' ('rich in vines') by Homer—which controlled the lucrative passage between the Euboean Gulf and the open sea. Its strategic location led Pericles to banish the Histiaeans and install 2,000 clerurchs here in 446 BC. The city became known thenceforth as *Oreos*, which appears to have been previously a deme of *Histiaea*, on a site very close by. After the banished Histiaeans were called back to their former city at the end of the Peloponnesian War, the city was subsequently known by both names. Its importance grew considerably through the 4th and 3rd centuries BC, until it was destroyed by the Romans in 199 BC. Its coinage circulated widely in the Aegean. According to Livy, *Oreos* had two citadels separated by a valley, hence the modern plural 'Oreoi': it possessed a maritime acropolis, which dominated the port—now the site of the castle—and an inland acropolis, *Oreos Apanos*. The city had fortification walls, a planned and prosperous public area, and extensive cemeteries. As a bishop's seat since as early as the 5th century, Oreí remained the centre of Northern Euboea through Byzantine times. A prosperous, small town existed under the Ottomans, which came under the rule of Ali Pasha, the 'Lion of Ioannina', in the late 18th century. After his assassination in 1822, the area was important as the scene of some of the first battles in the Greek War of Independence.

Modern Istiaia (4km inland) received numerous refugees from Asia Minor: the new settlement of Aghios Giorgios, 1km south of the town, was built for them.

The attractively laid out town, planned in 1833 by the Bavarian architect, Georg Schumayer, probably follows the ancient street plan. In the harbour, the submerged line of the **ancient mole** can be made out. A little behind the church of the Sotir by the shore, stands the *'**Bull of Oreí**' (late 3rd century BC)—a bold and remarkably preserved piece of Hellenistic funerary sculpture, found by the shore in 1965. The beautiful definition of the surface—of the tail, and especially around the neck and shoulders—is achieved by extensive and sensitive use of the claw chisel. The horns were fitted separately, and were possibly in a different material—bronze or ivory. Nearby is a small collection of column fragments and capitals from the ancient town: other vestiges can be seen *in situ* in the area between the shore and the acropolis.

Inland to the east of the shore rises the hill of **Kastro**—the ancient marine acropolis of Ancient *Oreos*—now crowned by the ruins of a Venetian fort, built over successive Byzantine and Hellenistic fortification walls which are visible in places below. An archaeologists' trench on the summit reveals yet earlier, ancient walls. In the northeast corner of the area are two tombs, one Hellenistic, one Early Christian. Below the castle to the southwest is the interesting church of **Aghios Basilios**: in the crypt, beneath an ungainly construction of the 1970s, are the remains of an **Early Christian place of worship** cut down into the rock, with a curious rock-hewn **niche** behind the altar forming the central liturgical focus. At the west end of the church is a bulky, **ancient sarcophagus** which was found close by, similar to those in the northeast corner of the Kastro site: it is said to have contained the remains of an early bishop of Oreí.

A little way inland, to the east of Oreí, lies modern **Istiaía** (16km) which has a number of fine old houses and middle-Byzantine churches—**Aghia Paraskevi** in the main square, and **Aghios Nikolaos** and **Aghii Pavlos and Petros** to the south and east of the square. Of these Aghios Nikolaos is the most interesting—as pleasing in form from outside as it is inside: a modern narthex leads into a low interior with three aisles and apses, supported in part on monolithic stone columns. The scattered remains of painted scenes inside are executed in the simplest and fewest of colours (local earth pigments); they are the work of local artists painting probably in the late 16th century. The town also has a small **Natural History Museum** with preserved specimens of marine and other fauna.

AROUND CAPE ARTEMISION

East of Istiaía the landscape becomes hilly and verdant. A branch to the left leads to the rural chapel of the **Panaghia Dinioús** in a setting of great tranquillity. Not far beyond the turning, the road touches the shore again at the villages of **Asmíni** (23.5km) and **Artemísio** (28km) where there are good shaded beaches. The village of Artemísio and the cape to the west both take their name from a shoreside temple of Artemis *Proseoia*, mentioned by Plutarch in his *Life of Themistocles* (VIII, 1)—surrounded, he says, by a wall of a kind of marble that imparted the odour and colour of saffron when rubbed. Plutarch always has intriguing anecdotes to relate. The ruins of the small 6th century Byzantine complex of Aghios Giorgios on an isolated spur of the hills east of Pevki and west of Gouves probably lie over the site of the ancient temple. It was here, in the **bay of Pevki**, that the Greek fleet based itself during the three days of crucial fighting in the straits, in which they succeeded in blocking the advance of the fleet of Xerxes, early in the second Persian invasion of 480 BC.

THE STRATEGY OF THE
BATTLE OF CAPE ARTEMISION

This first confrontation of Xerxes's invasion of 480 BC, between the Persian and Greek fleets, took place in July; at this stage, the strategy of the Greeks, who realised that an immediate and outright resistance to the advance of the Persian forces would be mistaken, was to try to hinder and delay their progress nonetheless. An army of the size of that assembled by Xerxes depended heavily on the reinforcement and provisioning afforded by the fleet which tracked its progress, keeping pace with it along the coast. The Greeks therefore aimed to do two things: first, to separate the Persian fleet from the army; and second, if possible, to send the fleet into the hostile and exposed waters along the east coast of Euboea, rather than allowing them access to the calm and inhabited shores of the inland gulf. Themistocles also needed time to prepare the evacuation of Athens, and the longer the Greeks could delay Xerxes—if possible into the early weeks of September—the greater pressure he would then be under to conclude his invasion before the changing season brought bad weather.

The story of the engagement at Artemision is told in detail by Herodotus (*Hist.* VIII, 1–23); his account makes fascinating and valuable reading. The losses were considerable on both sides and the outcome indecisive. But the overall Greek strategy was successful: those Persian ships which attempted the east coast of Euboea perished in bad weather and inhospitable waters; and the delay inflicted on Xerxes both here at Artemision and in the contemporaneous stand-off at Thermopylae across the water, cost him valuable time. It also gave vital breathing space for the Greeks to regroup and for Attica and Athens to prepare themselves for the inevitable onslaught. The psychological effect of the outcome cannot be overestimated: it showed to the Greeks that massive superiority of numbers on the Persian side did not necessarily prove invincible in the face of agile and intelligent strategic planning.

The villages of Asmíni, Artemísio and **Goúves** (29.5km) have many attractive wooden-balconied houses, similar in style to the architecture of the area of Mount Pelion across the water to the north. The idiosyncratic Ottoman **castle of Goúves**, built in the early 1800s by Ibrahim Ağa, which dominates the delightful village is constructed in a similar combination of materials with particularly fine wooden raftering. For a period it belonged to the Athenian poet, Giorgios Drosinis (1859–1951); it now constitutes a small and interesting **Ethnographic Museum**.

The road climbs eastwards from Goúves and turns south at Agriovótano above **Cape Artemision** (*2km of track leads down to the point*). The cape not only gives its name to the important naval battle, but also to two of Greece's most spectacular underwater archaeological finds.

In 1926 the left arm of a bronze statue was found at the site of an **underwater shipwreck** which had occurred in the 2nd century BC in the waters off Cape Artemision. The site was properly examined in 1928 and the rest of the magnificent, mid-5th century BC bronze statue of *Zeus* hurling a thunderbolt (sometimes erroneously referred to as an image of Poseidon) was salvaged from the water. The work has since been tentatively attributed to Kalamis. In the same year, the first fragments of another of the most famous bronzes of antiquity were also salvaged—the dramatic, Hellenistic group of the *Horse and Jockey*. A second search in 1936 found further fragments, sufficient to attempt a valid reconstruction of the group. The piece probably dates from the early 2nd century

BC. Both pieces may have been produced on the mainland—at Corinth or Sicyon—and were being transported to Pergamon when they were wrecked off the cape here: both are now in the National Museum of Archaeology in Athens.

THE NORTHEAST COAST

On the east shore south of cape Artemision, below the village of **Elliniká**, is the small harbour and promontory of **Aghios Nikólaos** (40km). This is probably the site of **Ancient *Helleniko***—where some of the Greek fleet may have provisioned before the Battle of Cape Artemision. The enclosed bay looks across to the Pelion peninsula and Skiathos, with the little islet and chapel of Aghios Nikolaos just off-shore. The ancient settlement was to the east side, and evidence shows that the headland was fortified. A number of ancient architrave and other blocks have been collected in the field beside the low saddle of the promontory.

The wealth of surface finds scattered over this whole stretch of the northeast edge of the island suggests that there was an extensive network of forts and settlements protecting and surveying the important sea passages through these waters, especially from Archaic to Hellenistic times.

South from Elleniká the landscape becomes steeper
and more densely forested. There are fine beaches below
Vasiliká (46km), and east of Aghia Anna (67km) where
a road leads down to the long, sandy bay at **Agali**. The
north end of the bay is sheltered by the promontory of
Aghios Vasilios where the remains of ancient fortification
have been tentatively identified as belonging to the ancient town of *Trychas*. The area to the northwest of Aghia
Anna, stretching as far as **Kerasiá** and beyond it to the
west, is the location of a fossilised forest dating from the
Upper Miocene era, 10–25 million years ago—a period
when a continuous land mass connected this area to Anatolia. It has yielded significant evidence of early fauna: examples of early ungulates, both *Perissodactyla* (elements
of the skulls of rhinoceri bearing two horns) and of *Ar-
tiodactyla* (such as a kind of short-necked giraffe) are at-
tested.

AROUND LIMNI AND PROKOPI—
CENTRAL NORTHERN EUBOEA

(*Limni = 0.0km for distances in this section*)

Gathered in front of a south-facing shore surrounded by hills and with beautiful views across the water into Boeotia and Phthiotis, **Limni** is an attractive centre from which to explore the rural areas of northern central Euboea. Spirited, yet pleasingly tranquil; understated, but quietly elegant; the town has conserved much of the dignified architecture and planning of its late 19th century design. Wrought-iron balconies supported on finely carved marble volutes, balustrades, and coloured neoclassical façades combine in a variety of styles: none exaggerated; all interesting. Little remains of Ancient *Elymnion* to which Limni is the modern successor. The earliest vestiges are to be found at the curious **church of the Panaghítsa** which stands in a small square about three blocks inland and to the right of the '*Eirinidikteio*' building on the waterfront next to the statue of Lela Karayiannis—a martyr of the underground resistance movement in Greece during the Second World War.

The church looks more like a low, squat house, with a single apsidal extension in its northeast corner: the row of small columns to its north survive from an Early Byzantine predecessor on this site, believed to date from the reign of Justinian in the 6th century and destroyed 200 years later by Saracen raiders. In the interior is an area of late Roman **mosaic floor** from an ancient bathing complex. In the floor of the apse, visible through two low arches, the mosaic has decorative **representations of fish and marine animals** which, given their importance also as Christian symbols, may explain the construction of the church over this area of the Roman baths in the first place. A marble statue of Hercules (now in the museum in Chalcis) was found on the site in 1856: more floor-mosaic and other later finds are in the local museum and the Byzantine Museum in Athens.

At the opposite end of the water-front, set back from the northern extremity of the beach and cut into the cliff-face, is the 11th century **hermitage of Hosios Christódoulos**. Here tradition relates that Christódoulos (*see vol. 15, 'Northern Dodecanese'*), the founder of the Monastery of St John on Patmos, died in March 1093 after he had been forced to flee from Patmos to Euboea in the face of Turkish incursions. The interior, filled with censers and icons, is a minute grotto of appropriately hermitic simplicity.

The other churches of the town, often richly decorated and furnished, date mostly from the last 130 years. A small and orderly **Municipal Museum** (*open summer Mon–Sat 9–1, Sun 10.30–2, week-days only in winter*) exhibits a collection of ancient and Byzantine antiquities found locally, as well as examples of local costume, furniture and domestic articles, in the setting of a restored Limniot house of the late 19th century, in which the original disposition of the rooms has been respected. Notable are: (*ground floor*) the large area of mosaic from the Late Roman baths by the church of the Panaghitsa (*see above*); some fine Hellenistic and Byzantine coins; a carved Roman family *stele*; and memorabilia of two Limniot patriots—Angelis Govios and Lela Karayiannis. On the *upper floor* are well-selected and presented examples of local costume, textiles, furniture and lace-work.

The scenic continuation of the shoreline road to the *southeast*, passes by the former magnesite minehead and loading-bays at **Katounia** (3km), once operated by the Anglo-Greek Magnesite Co. In the early part of the 20th century the mine processed around 35,000 tons of raw material per year. Today the defunct buildings have become dwellings immersed in flowering vegetation. The mine owner's house later became the residence of the translator and scholar, Philip Sherrard (1922–95), who constructed the small stone church of Aghia Skepi in the valley in 1993. The road passes along an attractively wooded shore and ends below the western face of **Mount Kandili** (Ancient Mount *Aigai*: 1,236m) which drops over 600m sheer into the water, dispatching strange currents of wind onto the waters below. Here, set back from the shore and tucked into the lee of the mountain is the 16th century *convent of Aghios Nikólaos Galatáki (9km) (*open summer 9–12, 5–8; winter 4–7*) first founded purportedly on the site of a temple of Poseidon in the 8th century. The dedication to St Nicholas, patron saint of mariners, may be a carry through from the cult of Poseidon, divinity of the waters.

The perfectly maintained nunnery has a compact form dominated by the sturdy **tower** (now sleeping quarters for guests) built between 1555 and 1562 by Hosios David Gerontos as a defence against pirate raids. A number of marbles, amongst them a fine fragment of an Ionic capital— evidence of an earlier, ancient presence in the area—have been collected together in the courtyard. The *catholicon* was built in 1566: the dome is supported by four columns, which on the south side have early capitals—one Ionic, the other early Byzantine. The walls have **areas of wall-painting** which were executed in 1586; their surface has been chipped to facilitate the adherence of a subsequent layer of plaster for later paintings, which were then lost when the building suffered a fire in the 18th century. The best preserved and most complete paintings, figuring scenes of the miracles of St Nicholas, are in the narthex which is roofed with six blind domes. The '*Ladder of ascent to Heaven*' on the south wall is particularly noteworthy. The later wall-paintings in the ***parecclesion*** on the south side, dedicated to the Baptist, are in good condition, and include decorative details such as the unusual guinea-fowl depicted below the window in the south wall. At several points graffiti of boats have been scratched into the surface of the wall as votive acknowledgements to St Nicholas by grateful mariners. About 200m east of the convent, through the rear door, is the hermitage and cave chapel of St Andrew, with faint remains of painting: the convent conserves the hand of St Andrew as a relic.

ROVIES AND ITS HINTERLAND

The new coast road *northwest* from Limni to Aedipsos, reaches **Roviés** after 10km, set back behind a wooded shore of great beauty near to the site of Ancient *Orobiai* which, according to Thucydides (*PW*. III. 89), was destroyed by a seismic tsunami in 426 BC. The centre is dominated by the mediaeval **Frankish tower** built by

Guillaume de Villehardouin, Prince of Achaea, between 1255 and 1258, during his successful war against the Venetian lords of the island. The tower—now disfigured by concrete additions—was a possession of the Benaki family in recent times. From Roviés a pleasant loop can be made into the forested landscape of the interior in order to visit the 19th century **monastery of Hosios David Gerontos** which is a much-frequented centre of local pilgrimage and has wall-paintings which were executed in the first years of this century. A loop can be made via the gorge and **waterfalls of Drymona**, returning once again to Roviés, via the picturesque village of **Kokkinomyliá**.

AROUND KIRINTHOS

The main road to the south of the island climbs inland to the east from Limni: shortly before the watershed, amongst the trees to the left of the road, is the church of the **Panaghia** which, though much restored, is a 15th or 16th century foundation. A fragment of wall-painting survives underneath the outside steps at the southeast corner. There is evidence of an ancient **marble quarry** on the crest of the hill at Mesopetri: running-drill and wedge cuts can be seen in the native rock about 80m east of the summit. Much of the fertile land to the south of the road between Myrtiás and Kechriés (10km) was part of the purchases made in the 19th century by the Noel family (*see below*); the village of **Farákla** (14km) is a good example of the kind of planned settlement and stone farmbuildings which they built and is architecturally of a piece with the main house at Prokopi. At **Strofiliá** (13.5km) the Limni road joins the principal north/south road of the island. The town's main church of Aghia Triada (1879), though not of architectural interest, possesses a remarkable, **painted wooden iconostasis**, typical of a late 19th century vernacular style.

The attractively wooded village of **Kirinthos** (18.5km) takes its name from nearby Ancient *Kerinthos*, although the village itself was only created in the 1830s around the stately **Villa Averoff** (*see lodging p. 142*) at its centre. The remains of *Kerinthos* are 5km to the east on the coast at 'Kastrí', close to the tiny resort of Krya Vrysi.

Ancient *Kerinthos* lies at the east end of the beach, beyond the fast-flowing Voudoros Stream, which narrows sufficiently by the sea to permit fording. Directly beyond this, a series of walls confront you, which were the western limit of the settlement—an **outer enceinte** in large, polygonal blocks whose masonry is that of the 6th century BC, with an inner wall constructed of smaller elements behind it. The site is oblong in shape and extends over three successive rises, terminating at the eastern end in a natural precipice. The **base of a small temple**, oriented to the cardinal points, can be detected at the highest point above this eastern limit. The line of the fortifications running east along the north side is clear, with the base of a **bastion** clearly visible; to the south, the ruins (mostly walls of Hellenistic construction) are immersed in undergrowth which covers the slope down to a basin of fertile fields which would in antiquity have been a protected area of water, possibly used as a **harbour** and linked to the sea below the western walls of the city. The remains of **public buildings** of the Hellenistic era, bordering a wide street, have been laid bare on the saddle between the central and western hills. The overall plan seems regular and oriented to the cardinal points, and therefore of Hippodamian inspiration. *Kerinthos* drew considerable wealth from the fertile land of its interior in the plain watered by the Kireas River. It figures in the Homeric catalogue of ships, and is mentioned by Strabo: early on, probably in the 5th century BC, it lost its independence to *Histiaia*.

Mandoudi (21km) stands in the low land at the mouth of the valley of the **River Kiréas**, which nurtures several kilometres of plane-tree woods to the south. Three kilometres south of Mandoudi, opposite the church of the

Koimisis tis Theotokou, a small sign points east to the '**Megalos Platanos**' ('Great Plane'): 800m down the east side of the river is this vast and remarkable vegetable—perhaps one of the oldest plane-trees in Europe—now slowly dying.

PROKOPI

After 30km from Limni you come to **Prokopi**, whose often busy activity centres on the large church of **Aghios Ioannis Roussos**, 'St John the Russian'—the town's miracle-working patron saint. 'Prokopi' is the name that Greek refugees coming from Ürgüp (a Turkish corruption of the Greek '*Prokopion*') in Cappadocia gave to this village when they arrived here in the mid 1920s. As well as a name, the refugees brought with them the body and relics of their guardian saint, a hermit and healer, born in Russia in 1690 and taken as a captive to central Anatolia in 1711 during the wars between the Sultan and Peter the Great. He died in Ürgüp in 1730 at the age of 40. His presence in the church in Prokopi is the focus of an active and widespread cult which culminates on his feast day, 27 May. The relics—including the saint's beret which the faithful still put on their heads when they visit—are in the small chapel on the left on entering: further inside the church on the left is the enbalmed body. Up until the arrival of the refugees, Prokopi was known by its Ottoman name, 'Ahmetağa'. Its recent history is closely intertwined with the Noel family, relatives of Byron, who purchased the surrounding land in the 1830s and whose manorhouse—in a curious hybrid of Greek, colonial, *hacienda*, and English suburban styles—overlooks the village from a wooded hill to the northwest.

THE NOELS ON EUBOEA

The 'Konaki' mansion and its extensive lands at what was then called 'Ahmetağa' (now Prokopi) were purchased in 1832 by Edward Noel, a prominent Philhellene, painter, poet and relative of Byron's wife, from whom he borrowed money to buy the estate from a departing Ottoman official, Ismail Bey, at the time when the independence of Euboea was being negotiated. Turkish landowners were allowed to sell their estates before leaving, and the Greek Government under Capodistrias encouraged foreigners to purchase their lands. Edward Noel was an idealist and came to Greece with the ambition of helping to restore the country to its former (ancient) glory—in his case, by transforming the local economy of Euboea and establishing a modern agricultural college. Roads, mills, dams, stone houses for the agricultural workers, and a church were all built under his aegis.

When the Canadian-born Philip Baker married Edward Noel's grand-daughter who had inherited the estate in 1919, the family changed its name to Noel-Baker. Philip Noel-Baker was an Olympic athlete and later a Labour Member of Parliament who served in several cabinets. He received the Nobel Prize for Peace in 1959 for his work on disarmament. Since his death in 1982 the estate has been owned by his son, Francis Noel-Baker, also a former Labour Member of Parliament. Possession of the land has, from the outset, been repeatedly challenged by the Greek Government. Co-existence with the local community has also often been problematic: the issue of the desecration of family graves by locals became the subject of a parliamentary exchange in the House of Lords during Margaret Thatcher's second government. Virginia Woolf and Maria Callas are among the writers and artists who have been guests at the *Konaki*.

AROUND PROKOPI: DAFNOUSA (WEST); PILI AND SARAKINIKO (EAST); & PAGONDAS (SOUTH)

Prokopi is at the meeting-point of several roads. To the west, a road leads towards the eastern slopes of Mount Kandili, densely forested in mature Aleppo pines. Two kilometres beyond the village of **Dafnousa** (4km from Prokopi), formed by Slav settlers, is the large **Venetian tower mansion of Bezas** (*the track south of Dafnousa, then west, climbs up beneath it*). Beyond and to the north lies the area which was most actively mined for magnesite around the turn of the 20th century—now amply reclaimed by forest.

From just south of Prokopi centre, a branch-road leads to the east coast, touching the shore at the crescent bay of **Píli** (42km). A few metres before the harbour, to the left of the road, is the tiny mid-14th century church of **Aghios Ioannis Theologos**, whose single-vaulted interior is completely covered with later **wall-paintings**, which in places are hard to read because of a layer of dirt and soot. A particular curiosity is the bizarre frieze of hellish tortures depicted in a running frieze, low on the south wall: some of the artist's inventions are worthy of Bosch.

Beyond Píli, a *scenic road climbs a further 10km along the coast to **Vlachiá** and to **Sarakíniko** (52km). The forested massif of Mounts Pixariás (1326m) and—more distantly—Dírfys (1743m) towers to the inland side and the road is bordered by magnificent pines. Most of these trees will necessarily date from after the last major fire 50 years ago; but a number of very impressive specimens predate that. The small bays are frequently backed with majestic plane-trees and, off-shore, the coastline is given interest and beauty by tiny rocky islets. The wild east coast of the island can be followed further from here, but the road is sometimes poor and a resilient vehicle is required.

The main road south from Prokopi enters a narrow defile, shortly after the wayside church of Aghios Giorgios (34.5km), and climbs steadily through densely forested gorges for the next 11km to the summit of the pass (609m) which affords *magnificent views towards the Sporades. In these landscapes it is possible to understand the enthralment that Edward Noel and his contemporaries felt when they first visited this area, referring to it as the 'Greek Switzerland'.

Shortly before the summit a branch road leads to **Pagóndas** (48km), and beyond to Markátes, small mountain communities immersed in steep pine-forests. To the

south of Pangondas are the Larko Nickel- and Iron-ore
Mines.

(*The southern descent of this road to Psachná and Chalcis is
covered in the next section, at pp. 66–67.*)

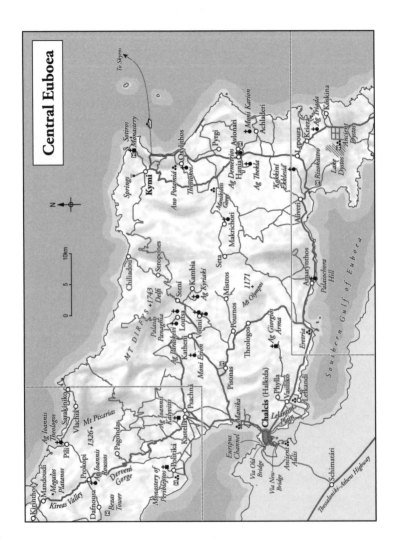

Central Euboea

CHALCIS (HALKIDA), ERETRIA & AMARYNTHOS

(Chalcis = 0.0km for distances in this section)

Chalcis—'Halkida' in demotic Greek, and 'Negroponte' to the Venetians—is the capital of the *nome* of Euboea. Busy, historically important and beautifully sited on both sides of one of the most curious channels of sea water in the Aegean, the city itself and its architecture—built and rebuilt after countless earth tremors and sprees of destruction—would win few beauty contests. Although there is now a new suspension bridge that spans the channel for through traffic, any exploration of Chalcis needs to start at the old bridge over the Euripus: it was this that gave the city life, significance and wealth, as well as two harbours and dominance of one of the most lucrative trading hubs in Greece after Corinth and the Piraeus.

Chalcis was throughout antiquity the chief city of Euboea. Its position, controlling the narrowest point of the Euripus channel and the principal crossing to the mainland (first bridged in 411 BC) with harbours both north and south of the city, destined it to considerable commercial importance. It is probable that the city's main economic resource was bronze-working and that the name 'Chalcis' (from χαλκός, meaning copper) reflects the preeminence of that industry. Because of continuous subsequent occupation of the same site, little of the ancient city has survived: there are some remains from the Late Geometric period, but little is known of the exact whereabouts of the earlier Mycenaean city of the 'big-hearted ... Elephenor' and of his 'swift Abantes' of which Homer speaks (*Iliad* II, 536–540). The city was a busy and influential commercial hub, handling and trading the raw materials produced in North and Eastern Greece and in the Black Sea area (timber, grain, salt-fish, precious metals etc.) which were headed to Athens, Corinth and the Peloponnese, against the finished products, pottery, and olive oil, which returned from those centres back up the same trade-routes. Chalcis did not just trade, however, it set about energetically securing the trade routes for itself by planting a wide diaspora of colonies along them. Few Greek cities, in proportion to their size, could have given rise to a greater number of colonies than Chalcis—so many on the Macedonian peninsula between the Thermaic and Strymonian gulfs that the whole peninsula was called 'Chalcidice' (mod. '[C] *Halkidiki*'). It also pushed far to the west in the Mediterranean, settling its inhabitants and interests in Sicily—at Naxos, and Messana (Messina)—and on mainland Italy—at Rhegion (Reggio Calabria) and Cumae. Cities were often forced to colonise when their population became too great for the available resources or supply of fresh water at home; this can scarcely have been the case at Chalcis, and the instinct to colonise so extensively here must be put down to the remarkable ἐμπορικό πνεῦμα—the 'entrepreneurial spirit'—of its citizens.

Another defining element may have been the city's constant struggle with nearby Eretria (only 20km away) for possession of the fertile Lelantine plain which lay between them. This was not just an idle local struggle, but a bitter war which dragged on for decades in the second half of the 8th century BC, and involved a number of other Greek city-states as distant as Miletus (which supported Eretria) and Samos (which supported Chalcis). The outcome is not altogether clear, although Chalcis appears subsequently to have controlled the plain in the 7th century BC. The city's last king, Amphidamos, who was a contemporary of Hesiod, was killed in this struggle. Afterwards the government passed to the aristocracy (although Aristotle in his *Politics* cites a later tyrant named Phoxus, who is otherwise unknown.) After the city sided with Boeotia against Athens in an attempt to reinstate the exiled tyrant Hippias, the Athenians overwhelmed the city in 506 BC, confiscated and settled clerurchs on their territory, dismantled their navy and took control of their Italian and Sicilian colonies. According to Herodotus,

Chalcis contributed 20 ships in 480 BC to the Greek fleet at Salamis and its soldiers took part in the battle of Plataea. Demosthenes saw Chalcis as instrumental in extending Macedonian attempts to control Greece. The city was taken in 338 BC by Philip of Macedon, who settled a garrison on the mainland side of the Euripus. In the 2nd century BC it was largely under Roman control, and was attacked punitively in 146 BC (in the same year that Corinth was also razed by the Romans) for disloyalty during the struggle between Rome and the Achaean Confederacy.

In the 6th century AD, the Emperor Justinian had an innovative, movable bridge constructed on the Euripus to increase the ease of passage for commerce. The city appears to have maintained a discreet commercial importance throughout the Byzantine period, with the production and trade of silk becoming a new and increasinlgy important element of its economy. In 1210 Chalcis was seized by the Venetians, who fortified it with walls and made it the capital of their kingdom of Negroponte. The name 'Negroponte' is an Italian variant on '*Egripo*' or '*Evripo*'. With considerable expense of military energy the Turkish forces of Mehmet the Conqueror took the city in 1470, built their first castle of Karababa over the Venetian fort, and Chalcis became the headquarters of the Kaptan Paşa. The Venetian admiral and doge, Francesco Morosini, tried to regain the city in 1688 but had to call off his siege after 4,000 of his troops died of malaria. The city was only freed of Turkish control in 1833 when the whole island of Euboea became part of the independent Greek state.

The mainland approach via the old road to the Euripus is guarded by the **Karababa** ('black father') **Castle**, the fortress greatly amplified by the Turks in 1686; vestigial cuts in the rock suggest an ancient fortress on this site, possibly the Macedonian fort built in 334 BC. The walls give a comprehensive view of the strait and the whole town. The unusual bridge (1962) that carries the old road over the Euripus, opens by a double action; the carriageway descends just sufficiently to allow the two half-spans to roll on rails under their own approaches. The channel is only 38m wide at this point.

THE EURIPUS

The Euripus is the name given to the narrow stretch of water which separates the land mass of Euboea from the mainland of Greece at its closest point, where it is less than 40m from the Boeotian coast. Islands always form barriers to the tidal movement of waters, but the effect is generally not immediately apparent unless that barrier is particularly long (e.g Jura in the

Hebrides) and/or confines a narrow area of water against the mainland (e.g the Isle of Wight). Euboea falls egregiously into both categories, and its considerable length means that the (albeit small) tidal fluctuations up the Euboean channel from the south end, and those down the channel from around the northern end of the island are separated by an appreciable period of time. The resultant effect at the narrowest point of the Euripus is therefore highly anomalous, giving rise to alternating currents, which can change direction as often as six or seven times a day. The current flows from north to south for about three hours at a rate which can vary between 6 and 12 knots. It then suddenly subsides; and, after a few minutes of quiescence, it begins to flow again in the opposite direction. These currents are driven by the gradient which forms between the respective water-levels to either side of the narrows, caused by the restriction of tidal movement at the bottleneck in the strait. Tides in the Mediterranean are weak by comparison with those in the open ocean; but the considerable fluctuations in the depth of the sea-bed in the Euripus (an unusual element which it has in common with the treacherous straits of Corrievreckan off Jura), as well as the constriction of the channel help magnify their effect disproportionately at this point.

The exact mechanics and timing of the water flow are still not fully understood. Its behaviour was widely speculated on from ancient times. Socrates (*Phaedo*, 90) uses the variability of the Euripus as a metaphor for that which is in a constant state of flux. The phenomenon is alluded to by Aeschylus (*Agamemnon*, 190), as well as by Livy, Cicero, Pliny and Strabo. According to a frivolous popular tradition, Aristotle, in despair at his failure adequately to explain the phenomenon, is said to have flung himself into the Euripus.

Passage through the channel with the current can be dangerous and the bridge is opened only when the flow is favourable. The capricious narrows were first spanned in 411 BC by what appears to have been a wooden bridge. In 334 BC, Chalcis included the Boeotian fort of Kanethos (across the channel) within its city boundaries. In the 6th century AD, under Justinian, the fixed bridge was replaced by a movable structure to facilitate the movement of vessels. The

Turks then replaced this with another fixed bridge in the 15th century. In 1856 a wooden swing bridge was erected; this was superseded by the first iron swing bridge, built in 1896 by a Belgian company which enlarged the channel and demolished the Venetian fort that had guarded the approach. This gave place in 1962 to the existing structure. The new road bridge, two kilometres further south, was opened in 1993.

The original bridge leads into 'Kastro', the older part of Chalcis and the area of the Venetian town of Negroponte whose northern walls ran along the line of the modern Eleftherios Venizelos Avenue. Immediately to the left, across the bridge, is a modern metal sculpture by Carmelo Mendola, distantly inspired by the *Nike of Samothrace*. To the right (south), Kallia Street—more an alleyway—leads past an old, wooden-framed **Ottoman house**, whose protruding first floor is supported on gracefully curving beams: the doorway and the corner on the alleyway are embellished with carved decoration. One block to the east, stands the late 17th century, Ottoman **mosque of Emir Zade**. Although shorn of its minaret and lacking its three-domed, arcaded loggia on the entrance façade, the symmetric proportions of its prayer-hall surmounted by

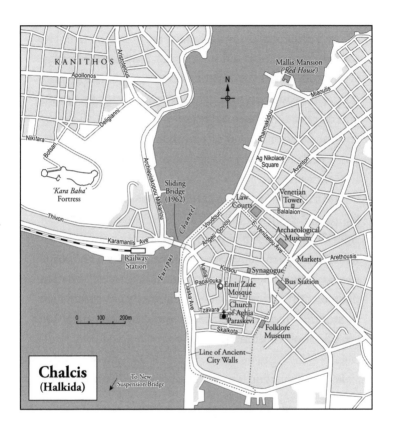

KANITHOS

Aristotelous

Apollonos

Botsari

Deligianni

Nikitara

'Kara Baba' Fortress

Thivon

Archiepiskopou Makariou

N

Mallis Mansion ('Red House')

Miaoulis

Pharmakidou

Ag Nikolaos Square

Avanton

Sliding Bridge (1962)

Channel

Euripus

Karamanlis Ave.

Railway Station

Voudouri

Argeni

Govio

Law Courts

Venetian Tower

Balalaion

E. Venizelou Ave.

Archaeological Museum

Markets

Arethousis

Kotsou

Synagogue

Bus Station

Kallia

Papalouka

Liaska Ave.

Emir Zade Mosque

Tzavara

Church of Aghia Paraskevi

Skalkota

Folklore Museum

Line of Ancient City Walls

0   100   200m

Chalcis (Halkida)

To New Suspension Bridge

a broad octagonal drum and dome are still attractive. The carved marble surround of the door has beautiful calligraphy and design. Substantially later in date is the more decorative **fountain** facing the mosque. Antique columns and capitals have been deposited in front of the building and the interior is used as a store for mediaeval antiquities. The 19th century synagogue of Chalcis is nearby on Kotsou Street.

From the southwest corner of the square of the mosque, Stamati Street leads towards the monumental church of **Aghia Paraskevi** which dominates an open area dotted with several venerable houses—one of which, opposite the west door of the church, bears a carved Venetian plaque with the Lion of St Mark above its entrance. Two monolithic Byzantine columns and capitals mark the west door of the church itself.

Recent scholarship (see: Pierre MacKay, *Ist. Ellen. Studi Byzantini ... di Venezia*, 2006) has shown that this was not a Byzantine cathedral church but was built as the Catholic priory church of St Mary of the Dominicans in the middle of the 13th century, as one of the early mission centres of the itinerant branch of the order. It probably occupies the site of a pre-existing Byzantine church which had fallen into disuse. It is an unusual (for Greece) example of early Dominican architecture, which has survived largely undamaged and little modified. The interior is grand and spacious, punctuated with *cipollino* and Hymettus marble columns (two of which are deeply fluted) surmounted by a variety of carved capitals. The chancel arch is carved with Gothic foliage and with the figures of St Dominic and St Peter Martyr. The heavy marble iconostasis was put up in the church in the last century, compromising the impressive sense of space the building would have possessed without it.

Two blocks to the east of Aghia Paraskevi, in a sombre military building erected by the Venetians, is the **Folklore Museum** (*open Wed 10–1, 6–8;Thur–Sun 10–1*) containing a small collection of fabrics, costumes, looms and musical instruments. To the north, at no. 43 Balalaíon Street, is the sole survivor of the many Venetian city-towers which marked the skyline of Negroponte in the 15th century. Unlike the rural mediaeval towers in Euboea, this has a ground-floor entry.

From the shore just to the north of the bridge, Venizélos Avenue leads southeast past the **neoclassical building of the Law Courts** ('*ΘΕΜΙΔΟΣ ΜΕΛΑΘΡΟΝ*') to the **Archaeological Museum** (*open daily 8.30–3, except Mon*) which, though small, is a collection of particularly high quality.

Much of the sculpture collection is in the courtyard and garden, with the best pieces disposed under two covered porticos. At the left end of Portico A is a ***marble panel** of the 2nd century BC, delicately carved with three rows of victorious athlete's laurel wreaths, with inscriptions (*IG XII* 9.952) at the centre of each wreath explaining the origin of the athlete and the nature of the contest won in the Games of the *Herakleia*: a good example of the beauty with which an essentially documentary list could be endowed in antiquity. Portico B has a choice selection of Hellenistic and Roman statuary in remarkably good state of conservation, including three 4th century BC **horse's-head** *protomes* from a monumental

cenotaph.

The interior is divided into three rooms: to *right* is Neolithic material from the Skoteini Cave, and Early Helladic pottery from Manika, including the characteristic, Early Cycladic, incised 'frying pans'. The Mycenaean artefacts include a bronze sword and pots which are exuberantly decorated with lily and vine-leaf designs. A rare, funerary group of Geometric **bronze figurines**—two humans leading a dozen oxen—comes from a grave at Dokos. The *central* room is dominated by the two Roman statues of Dionysos and an elegiac, heavy-headed, Antinous. To the right of the door is a particularly fine Roman **portrait bust of Polydeukion**, the favourite pupil and protégé—the 'Antinous', in other words—of the philosopher and philanthropist, Herodes Atticus. Opposite it is part of a pleasingly stylised, 5th century BC *relief of the sacrifice of a ram** from Larymna, whose carving is particularly delicate.

The room to *left* contains other sculptural pieces: two heads of archaic *kouroi* of the 6th century BC; three graceful attendants to Artemis from a sculptural group of the 4th century BC; several fine figurative grave *stelai*, and a votive relief, in excellent condition, unusually depicting the figure of **Hades together with Dionysos**. A central case exhibits a 1st century BC **gold wreath** belonging to a talented athlete: beside it is a **cup in clear glass** of the same period which has miraculously survived whole.

Not far (c. 600m) to the north of the museum, at the end of the first waterside promenade north of the bridge, is the Mallis family mansion, commonly know as the '**red house**'—a prominent neoclassical landmark, with fine marble door and window-frames, which is now a Municipal Cultural Centre.

To the east of the city-centre, the main north/south ring-road is traversed by the arcaded **Ottoman aqueduct**, which supplied Chalcis with water from two springs on the slopes of Mount Dírfys, 25km away.

NORTH OF CHALCIS

The main shore-road north from Chalcis leads through an unattractive commercial area which blends seamlessly with Nea Artaki. Just short of Nea Artaki (at 4km) a left turn leads down to the shore beside the promontory of **Mánika**. The flat, projecting tongue of land—or island, as it was then—the gentle shoreline and fertile land behind, constitute a familiar configuration of geography for early settlers. Although there is little to see here, this was the site of an important Early Helladic settlement (3rd millennium BC), the finds from which are to be seen in the museum in Chalcis (*Room 1*). Archaeological examination has centred on the neck of the tongue of land, but the extension of the settlement spread considerably inland.

At the junction in the road 11km from Chalcis, is the statue (1975) by Theodoros Papagiannis of Angelis Govios, hero and general of the Greek Independence revolution, who was born in Limni, and is buried in Psachná (church of Aghios Ioannis). The road splits here between the twin settlements of Kastélla and Psachná (13km). The right-hand branch passes through the centre of **Psachná**, 3km due north of which is the hill of **Kastrí** crowned by a Venetian castle, and 5km northeast of which is the monastery of the Panaghia Makrimalis. From **Kastélla**, the principal road continues towards the north of the island. After 3.5km a side-road heads east to the **monastery of Aghios Ioannis Kalyvitis**, dedicated to the 5th century Constantinopolitan saint, John Kalyvitis, the 'hut dweller'.

> The monastery buildings are new, but the *catholicon* is a small, freestanding, early 12th century church of considerable interest. Its upper areas have recently been restored, but the west door conserves its magnificent marble jambs, which are composed of four sections of *ancient entablature carved with an exquisite running frieze of palmettes. Other fragments, both ancient and Early Byzantine, are assembled in the area, some incorporated in the structure itself. The '*cloisonné*' brick- and stone-work in the church's three apses is particularly beautiful.

Beyond the junction for the monastery, the road north begins its long climb towards Pagondas, Prokopi, Limni (62.5km) and the north of the island (*see previous section*), offering wide views back over the Euboean Channel and Chalcis.

The road west from Kastélla skirts the coast and heads towards the attractive village of **Politiká** (20.5km), considered by some scholars to be the site of Ancient *Aigai* below the southeastern slope of the Mount Kandili massif. The skyline is dominated by a high 13th century **Frankish tower** whose south face incorporates several antique marble elements in the window-frames. The holes for fixing construction scaffolding are still clearly visible. Above the village is the **monastery of the Peribleptos** built around a small, domed, cruciform church originally constructed in the 11th century, though later rebuilt in the same form in the 17th century. Elements from the original structure are incorporated, such as the carved **marble cornice** over the west door. The interior is entirely decorated with 17th century **wall-paintings** of considerable character and interest, enlivened throughout by a brilliant red, minium pigment. The marble support of the iconostasis is also a good example of 17th century carving with elegant, Byzantine decorative motifs such as cypress, rosette and wreath.

SOUTH FROM CHALCIS

The road south leaves Chalcis through industrial outskirts between the shore and the hill of Vathrovoúni, whose western shoulder, overlooking the water, was the acropolis of Ancient *Chalcis*. The rich and fertile **Lelantine Plain**, recalled in the *Hymn to Apollo* for its lush vineyards, begins just beyond. In the 8th and 7th centuries

BC, the area was the subject of a deadly territorial rivalry between *Chalcis* and *Eretria*. The area's value was also appreciated in later epochs and the landscape is punctuated with several **Venetian towers and forts** which combined to guard its agricultural activity and inhabitants, as well as protecting the southern approaches to Chalcis. At the centre of **Vasilikó** (6km) is a well-preserved tower; there are two more between the villages of **Mýtikas** and **Phýlla** (8km); and a conspicuous castle above the latter, built on an ancient enceinte. The tower at Vasilikó was occupied by the Turks in 1470 during their siege of Negroponte.

An interesting detour east can be made from Phýlla to the **monastery of Aghios Giorgios Árma** (11km), a handsome stone church founded in 1141.

The form of the church is a compact and well-proportioned example of 12th century Byzantine architecture, and the combined silhouette of the two domed structures (*narthex* and *catholicon*) in one complex is cadenced and pleasing. The surrounding courtyard contains abandoned ancient columns and some strikingly carved scroll volutes. Other fragments are incorporated in the church: the decorative *anthemion* of a grave-*stele* is embedded in the wall above the west door; another sits over the east window, where it is combined with Byzantine decorative elements in marble

and fine brick-work which create a beautifully facetted en-
semble. The domed narthex, which was probably added at a
slightly later date, has darkened late-Byzantine wall-paintings. It is separated from the main, undecorated *catholicon*
by an intervening space and double-door. The cupola of the
main church is supported on columns (three of which are
ancient, and one fluted) with Ionic capitals. The unadorned,
stone architecture of the interior is striking.

LEFKANDI AND ERETRIA

From Vasilikó a by-road descends in 2km, through
a spreading area of suburban coastal residences, to
Lefkandí, site of one of the most significant *loci* of recent
archaeology in Greece.

The importance of Lefkandí lies in the fact that it has illumi-
nated a hitherto little understood period of early history—
referred to pejoratively as the 'Dark Age'—between the 11th
and 9th centuries BC. In precisely this period, Lefkandí, which
had nonetheless been inhabited from the Early Bronze Age,
became a particularly flourishing and important centre for
a wide area of Eastern Greece, the Islands, and the Eastern
Mediterranean. Then, around 700 BC, it was deserted and is
heard of no more. Lefkandí has been suggested by some as

the site of 'Old *Eretria*', the city Homer linked with Chalcis in the Catalogue of Ships, and which was the city Strabo saw and claimed (incorrectly) to be the city sacked by the Persians in 490 BC. Archaeological evidence has now shown that the city which the Persians destroyed was on the site of present-day Eretria.

The fascinating finds that come from Lefkandí are in the museum in Eretria (*see below*). On site there are two main points of interest—the **settlement** itself, where for the visitor there is little to see, and the remarkable *heroön* which lies a short distance away. The latter, however, should not be missed because of its considerable archaeological importance.

The **settlement** site lies a short walk from the south end of the main bay. The top of the flat headland of **Xeropolis** here was explored in 1965/66 and 1969/70 by the British School and found to be a settlement with three associated cemeteries. The excavations yielded unusually informative layers of Late Helladic IIIC through to Proto-Geometric material (12th to 10th centuries BC). The material suggests significant wealth, as well as clear commercial links with Cyprus and the Levant coast after the middle of the 10th century BC.

In a modern residential area, 200m uphill to the north of the harbour (between Chrysanthemon and Plateon Streets, on 'Toumba Hill'), are the remains of the *heroön, now cov-

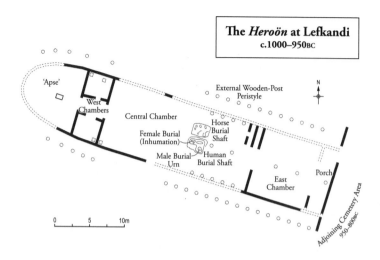

The *Heroön* at Lefkandi
c.1000–950BC

'Apse'

West Chambers

Central Chamber

Female Burial (Inhumation)

Male Burial Urn

Human Burial Shaft

Horse Burial Shaft

External Wooden-Post Peristyle

N

East Chamber

Porch

Adjoining Cemetery Area 950–800BC

0   5   10m

ered by a functional protective roof. These are the surface vestiges of what would have been a spacious and ambitious peripteral structure—the largest building of its period (c. 1000 BC) so far known in Greece. It was built of mud-brick on a high (1.5m) stone socle and measured about 14m wide by almost 50m long, with an apsidal end to the west and an entrance from the east. With internal and external wooden colonnades supporting a steeply raking roof, it represents a new form of monumental architecture and in many important aspects it prefigures later Greek temple design. In the main chamber was buried a man, a woman and four horses: the cremated remains of the warrior, wrapped in a fine cloth, had been placed in a bronze urn, together with the body of the woman surrounded by rich accoutrements. Unlike the warrior, the woman had not been cremated; the finding of a knife close to her head has led to speculation that she may have perished in a ritual sacrifice. It is particularly notable that the building was demolished in the same generation as it was constructed and deliberately covered with a mound, probably so as to form a hero-shrine to the deceased buried within.

Viewed in comparison with both the grandiose and much earlier constructions of Minoan and Mycenaean Greece and of what followed later in the Archaic period, the vestiges remaining at Lefkandí can seem less inspiring. But the monumentality of what is intimated here is remarkable for a period which has otherwise offered little that is of comparable size or complexity. It provides a crucial link in a possible continuity of architectural design between the Bronze Age and the historic period in Greece; it helps us to understand the design of the very earliest temples built at sites such as the *Heraion* on Samos and the pan-Aetolian sanctuary at Thermon on mainland Greece. But the fascinating questions the building raises about cultic practice in this important transitional period are more perplexing, since it cannot yet be established whether this building was originally constructed as a palace or '*megaron*' for the dignitaries later buried in it, or specifically as a place for honouring their passing, or even whether there was any primary divine aspect to the building and its cult which may have led to the burials under its roof.

From Lefkandí the coast road soon leads to **Erétria** (23km), 3km to the north of which are the ancient quarries (now reactivated) of the beautiful maroon-red and white **decorative marble**, known as *marmor chalcidicum* or 'Chalcidian marble' to the ancients, and as *Fior di pesco* ('peach flower') during the Renaissance.

The modern settlement of Erétria was founded as 'Nea Psará' in 1824 by refugees from the island of Psará. The new town overlies much of the city of **Ancient *Eretria*** whose ruins are the most extensive on Euboea.

As between siblings, proximity and similarity of position meant that the history of Eretria was intertwined with that of Chalcis its powerful neighbour only 20km to the north along the same coast—at times in close cooperation, at others in fratricidal conflict. Eretria's wealth grew from its exploitation of important maritime trade routes just as Chalcis's did, and the two cities participated together in the trade *emporion* of Al Mina on the Syrian coast: Eretria, like Chalcis, founded distant colonies in the 8th century—in the Northern Aegean, and on the islands of Corfu in the

Adriatic and Ischia in the bay of Naples. In the same period, however, the two cities came to blows over possession of the Lelantine Plain which lay between them, and it may have been Eretria's loss of that struggle which led to the abandonment of 'Lefkandí' (possibly Strabo's 'Old *Eretria*') in favour of the site now known as Ancient *Eretria*—although traces of Mycenaean, Proto-Geometric and Geometric occupation have been found on the acropolis above the site, suggesting a pre-existing occupation. The city of Miletus had come to the aid of Eretria in the Lelantine struggle, and it was perhaps for this reason that Eretria in turn joined Athens in supporting the Ionian revolt led by Miletus in the first years of the 5th century BC. In the revolt, Sardis —the Persians' regional capital—was razed by the Greeks. That conspicuous support cost Eretria dearly: when Darius invaded Greece is 490 BC, almost his first objective was the destruction of Eretria and the enslavement of its people.

The city recovered from the devastation and sent significant contingents to both the battles of Salamis in 480 and Plataea in 479 BC. Thereafter, in spite of a rebellion in 446 BC, the city was largely under Athenian control until it broke free in 411 BC, when Athens's attentions were elsewhere in the aftermath of the Sicilian débacle. In 377 BC it joined the Second Athenian Confederacy. Caught up in the intrigues between Athens and Macedonia, and subsequently between

Macedonia and Rome, it was sacked by the Romans in 198 BC. After a second destruction in 87 BC during the Mithridatic wars, the ancient city was never rebuilt.

The principal archaeological sites lie scattered to both sides of the main highway. A visit to them best begins at the excellent displays in the **museum** (*open daily 8.30–3, except Mon*) which stands just to the south of the road. The museum has two rooms: one dedicated to exhibits from prehistoric times to the beginning of the 6th century BC; the other containing the pedimental sculpture of the Temple of Apollo *Daphnephoros* and later Classical and Hellenistic pieces.

Room 1: the cases to the left exhibit the extraordinary finds from Lefkandí, bearing witness both to its wealth and the extent of its commercial trade overseas. Of particular note: the broad **alabastron** (*case 1*) in clay with magnificent **designs** of gryphon, deer and roe-buck in a light slip on dark background (c. 1100 BC); vases imported from Italy and Palestine; an elegant and un-threatening clay **centaur** (*case 3*), both man and horse, with fine Proto-Geometric decoration. This piece was curiously found broken in two halves and included in separate burials. Note also the **wheeled horse carrying two amphorae** (*case 4*), possibly a child's toy, of Attic origin; and the curious *cup, whose single handle which steadies the cup ingeniously ends in a leg wearing a fine laced boot. These pieces, which all date from the 11th and 10th centuries BC, show that, although surface decoration was mainly confined to pattern and geometric forms, there was an underlying ferment of creativity in plastic, figurative forms. *Case 5* exhibits simple but refined items of gold jewellery. The showcases to the right display a wide variety of pottery including a number of large, decorated **funerary *amphorae***, characteristic of the Geometric period. Amongst other items are imported artefacts from as far away as Syria, such as the 9th century BC **decorated horse-blinkers** fashioned in bronze (*case 12*).

Room 2 houses the sculpture fragments from the ***west pediment of the Temple of Apollo *Daphnephoros*** (*rear wall*), which date from the end of the 6th century BC. The scene, presided over by a central, standing figure of Athena with the Gorgon's head on her breast-plate, depicts Theseus carrying off Hippolyta (also called Antiope), Queen of the Amazons, on his shoulders. The predominantly 'Athenian' subject matter may reflect political connections between the two states. Lacking now the vibrant colours which once decorated their surface, the elements appeal to the eye even more intensely through their poise, clear forms, and elegant, rhythmic contours.

They are typical of the aristocratic art of the Late Archaic period. The showcases in the room exhibit objects mostly from Eretria in the Classical and Hellenistic periods—domestic items, votive burial offerings, Euboean coins (*case 16*), and **Panathenaic amphorae** awarded to athletic victors (*case 18*).

The modern highway almost exactly bisects the area of the ancient city. Points of archaeological interest lie to both north and south of the road.

To the *north* of the highway are:

The **West Walls and West Gate**. A circuit of nearly 4km of walls surrounded and protected the city, joining the acropolis hill in the northeast with the harbour in the southeast corner. The first enceinte was built (further to the east of the surviving walls) in the 8th century BC. The one visible here dates from c. 400 BC and is well-preserved, with the moat and the bases of external bastions extant along the western section of the excavated area, north of the highway. At the point where the ancient road from *Chalcis* entered the city is the **West Gate and Barbican**, constructed with a wide variety of kinds of masonry. The base of the walls in a tightly interlocking trapezoidal system is particularly impressive; the ample vaulted passage beneath that drained off the torrent

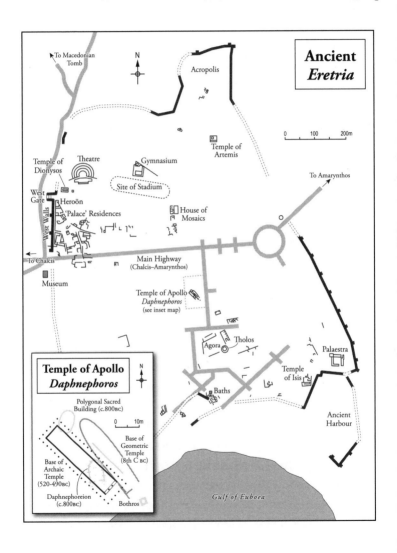

Ancient *Eretria*

To Macedonian Tomb

N

Acropolis

Temple of Artemis

0   100   200m

Temple of Dionysos

Theatre

Gymnasium

Site of Stadium

To Amarynthos

West Gate

Heroön

'Palace' Residences

House of Mosaics

West Walls

To Chalcis

Main Highway
(Chalcis–Amarynthos)

Museum

Temple of Apollo
Daphnephoros
(see inset map)

Agora   Tholos

Palaestra

Temple of Isis

Baths

Ancient Harbour

Gulf of Euboea

**Temple of Apollo
*Daphnephoros***

N

Polygonal Sacred
Building (c.800BC)

0   10m

Base of
Geometric
Temple
(8th C BC)

Base of
Archaic
Temple
(520-490BC)

Daphnephoreion
(c.800BC)

Bothros

is also finely constructed with a round arch at one end and a corbelled support at the other.

Directly inside and to the southeast of the West Gate are the remains of a small *heroön* in which were incorprated some noble-family tombs containing weapons and grave goods dating from the 8th century BC. At that time the *heroön* would have been outside the city walls which were only enlarged and moved further west in the late 5th century BC. In reaching this point on the site from the entrance to the archaeological area, you will have traversed an excavated area of large residences or so-called '**palaces**', some contiguous with the West Wall. There are several superimposed layers of construction in this area, but the houses at the highest level, mostly built around a central peristyle court, date from the late 5th and 4th centuries BC. A well-preserved clay bath remains *in situ* in one. Many different colours and types of stone were used for the threshold blocks.

To the northeast of the West Gate is the base of a 4th century BC **temple of Dionysos**, which was a Doric, peripteral structure with an altar which stood a short distance to the east. As is appropriate for Dionysos, the presiding divinity of drama, the precinct of his temple abuts the 5th century BC **theatre**, whose form is clear although it has largely been left covered by earth. It is curious that the natural slope of the acropolis hill to the east was not used to create the theatre, and that massive terracing had therefore to be undertaken to support its *cavea* on this flatter site. It retains its seven lower rows of seats, much defaced; the upper tiers, which were exposed to view, have nearly all been removed, block by block, to build the modern village. A semicircular drainage channel almost 2m wide runs in front of the lowest row. The design has unusual innovations: from the *orchestra*, steps descend through a square opening into an **underground vaulted passage**, leading to the *hyposkenion*; this was used for the sudden appearance and disappearance of agents of the underworld, as well as for the facilitating of special sound effects. The high stage is raised on seven or eight courses of masonry.

Further east, at the foot of the acropolis and above an area identified as the stadium, is a **Gymnasium** which was first excavated in 1895. By its west end was found an inscribed *stele* set up in honour of a gymnasiarch and benefactor. At the eastern extremity is an extensive series of water conduits which supplied the **bathing troughs**, still clearly visible along the side of a room with plain mosaic floor

Above the Gymnasium, paths lead up to the **acropolis** where the late 5th century BC enceinte and its well-preserved towers in isodomic masonry are visible, especially to the east side. On the way up are (left) remains of a *Thesmophoreion* (sanctuary to Kore and Demeter) and (right) the sanctuary of a female deity, perhaps Artemis *Olympia*. On returning once again towards the highway, you pass the '**House of the Mosaics**', recognisable because it is partly covered by a modern building and roof. This is a large and important residence—sometimes attributed to the philosopher Menedemos—constructed around 370 BC with a private area and an ample public area. Much of the furniture and small objects, including the exceptional terracotta Gorgon's head, which were found here are exhibited in the Museum (*Room 2, case 17*). The **figurative mosaics**—especially those in the middle reception room on the north side—are preserved *in situ*. They are executed mostly in black and white, and soberly highlighted with colour. The house appears to have been destroyed by fire a hundred years after it was built.

On a hill 1km west of the theatre, a tumulus encloses a **Macedonian tomb**. (*Key held by museum. Not signed. Take asphalt road parallel to west side of the archaeological area; then first fork left. Road climbs; as it turns sharply right, the tomb is at the summit of the hill crowned with pines.*) The neatly cut *dromos* on the north side leads to a square vaulted chamber containing two funeral couches in marble, with their pillows and draperies, two thrones and a table, all once coloured. A funerary sculpture—a lion or a sphinx—would have marked the grave from above.

To the *south* of the main highway:

The **temple of Apollo *Daphnephoros*** is Eretria's most significant monument, and was always the hub of the ancient city. (*East on highway, then last street south before the roundabout.*) Now that the Archaeological Department has recovered with earth most of the recent excavations, all that is visible is the large crepidoma of the Doric peripteral temple, erected c. 530/520 BC, to which the pedimental sculpture in the museum originally belonged. It had 6 x 14 columns, with a *cella* articulated in three aisles divided by a double row of columns. Noteworthy is the beautiful dressing of the blocks of the lowest level, which possess their natural irregular profile underneath, and are finished to a perfect, flat, lipped ledge on the upper surface. Below what is seen however, archaeologists have identified two earlier buildings: the first, dating from c. 800 BC, was an apsidal '***Daphnephoreion***', perhaps designed to imitate the early 'hut' of laurel branches which traditionally stood at Delphi; the second, built over it in the mid-7th century BC, was a longer building, again terminating in a wide apse at the northwestern end, with six (wooden) columns on the ends and 19 down each side. In plan and design this building has affinities with the *heroön* at Lefkandí and with the early *hekatompedon* at Samos. It lies partially under the north edge of the visible temple base.

Three other points of interest lie further to the southeast.

A meticulously cut, circular base with a central circular pit is visible in an area occupied by the ancient *agora*. This ***tholos*** dates from the 4th century BC and is possibly also the sanctuary of, or monument to, a hero. Beyond it, on what was the edge of the harbour in ancient times are the **baths** of the 4th century BC, probably belonging to a gymnasium complex. To the east of these are the ruins of a **temple of Isis**, whose cult was introduced into the Greek world by mariners and merchants returning from Egypt. The broken cult statue in terracotta was found *in situ* when the building was excavated in 1917.

AMARYNTHOS

A number of the early Helladic artefacts in the museum at Eretria come from excavations in the area of **Amárynthos** (33.5km) which was an important centre in Antiquity lying on the coast further to the east, where there was a sanctuary to Artemis *Amarysia*. A kilometre and a half beyond the eastern limit of the town is the **hill of Palaiochora**, between the main road and the shore, which in antiquity was a site of significant habitation from prehistoric through to Classical times. Today it is crowned by two 12th century churches. Both churches have the characteristic Euboean design with rectangular floor plan, and an elevated transverse barrel-vault in the ceiling to create the crossing. Closest to the water is the church of the **Koimisis tis Theotokou**, which has wall-paintings of considerable quality, but in poor condition; the church of the **Metamorphosis**, close by to the landward side, has no painting, but the simple dignity of the design is revealed in the plain stone interior. To the north, beside the road between Amárynthos and Ano Váthia, half way between the churches of Aghia Markella and Aghios Giorgios, is a Macedonian tomb of the 4th century BC.

AROUND MOUNT DIRFYS &
MOUNT OLYMPOS

This section covers a large rural area, stretching between, and to either side of, the two peaks of Central Euboea—Mount Dírfys (1,743m) the island's highest mountain, and the gentler Mount Olympos (1,171m) to its south. The area is one of the loveliest landscapes in the Aegean Islands. It is dotted with castles, mediaeval churches, springs, gorges and simple villages, forested with many varieties of trees, and generously watered. This is also an area rich in flora and fauna. The geography suggests no obvious itinerary: so the points of interest have simply been grouped and listed instead. For convenience, we propose making a base at Stení as a pleasant centre from which to explore the area.

(*Stení = 0.0km for distances in this section*)

Stení (26km from Chalcis) is an attractive village of balconied houses and stone dwellings—old mixed unselfconsciously with new—in a valley of plane-trees at the mouth of the pass across the east shoulder of Mount Dírfys. At c. 600m a.s.l. it remains pleasantly cool in the summer months. There is a delightful square shaded with planes, and the sound of running spring water is everywhere.

The mountain

Above the village, the road climbs rapidly and unrelentingly to the watershed through forests of chestnut, pine, spruce, wild cherry and plane. At the top (8.5km, c. 1,000m a.s.l.)—still heavily forested and scented with pine—the views are magnificent into Boeotia and towards Mount Parnassus, and over the east coast towards Skyros. The bald, conical peak of **Mount Dírfys** (1,743m) rises clear to the northwest. The mountain's presiding deity was Hera, who assumed the epithet '*Dirphya*'. A track climbs from the ridge to the northwest above the treeline to the Fountain of Liri Refuge (*36 beds. Information from: E.O.S. Halkidas, 22 Angeli Goviou, 34 100 Halkida, T. 22210 25230*). From the refuge a path which is marked all the way leads to the long ridge of the summit in under two hours.

The top of Dírfys is largely convex in relief, i.e. it does not have the convoluted form with protected rifts and gorges which characterises the summits of Mount Parnassus and Mount Olympus (the Great) and which create rare microclimates rendering their flora so diverse. Notwithstanding there are several endemic species, such as the rare *Minuartia dirphya*, a kind of sandwort—which grows on the northern slopes of the mountain around the 900–1,000m altitude, in small mat-like cushions—recognisable by its starburst of long, woody stems tipped with the modest, white flower. Also at the higher altitudes and on the escarpments there are fritillaries, aubretia (*Aubretia deltoides*) and *Viola delphinantha*.

The road descends tortuously on the northern side to **Strópones** (16.5km), with many traditional stone houses, continuing beyond through magnificent scenery to the isolated shore at **Chiliadoú** (29km).

The lower slopes

To the southwest of Mount Dírfys extends a wide, sloping apron of watered valleys which settle into a folded landscape, with something of the appearance of the rural areas inland of San Francisco in Northern California. In mediaeval times this fertile landscape was parcelled out amongst local feudal lords—hence the many Frankish and Venetian towers which punctuate the area, as for example at **Pisónas** (a particularly well-preserved example) in the west, and at Amithéa and Pyrgos, further east.

Around Kambia

The springs which rise beneath the mountains were often in antiquity the pretext for erecting small shrines to the Nymphs and other deities. These later became churches: then, close to them, more chapels and churches were built in their own right. The area of **Kambia** (4.5km south of Stení via Káto Stení) is especially rich in both water and churches. In the densely wooded valley above the village there is a trout farm today. The rising water here was collected by an **aqueduct** in Antiquity: at the southwest corner of the gorge, a deep, natural split in the rock face has been dressed and enlarged to form a water conduit (*best seen from the road that descends the east side of the valley below Kambia*). At **Aghia Kyriakí** (5km below Kambia), by a waterfall beneath mature planes, the church is built into a cave: only the south and west sides are constructed, and the apse is embedded in the natural rock. An *aghiasma*, or pool of sacred water, is cut into the north side of the floor, behind which the rushing of an underground stream can be heard.

Around Loutsa

The wide area below Dírfys is dotted with 12th–14th century rural churches, many with painted interiors. Several lie in the area of **Loutsa** and Katheni (6 and 8km respec-

tively west from Stení). In Loutsa, follow the road which
drops down southwest of the church of the Theotokos in
the main square for 600m to find the 13th century church
of **Aghia Paraskeví**—a small and isolated, barrel-vaulted
chapel with three arches, heavily buttressed to the south
side. (*The door is opened by pulling the wire to the right
hand side.*) In the fine 16th century **paintings** in the interior, there is an impressive array of saintly physiognomies
along the lateral walls, surmounted by narrative scenes;
the clearest paintings are on the west wall where the *Last
Judgement* unfolds in every detail, with the presence of
the Almighty represented by the small window through
which the light enters the church, and from which a river
of fire descends. This simple but poetic device—symbolising the presence of the Almighty by an opening with
natural illumination—is a pleasing example of the hum-
ble ingenuity of these rural Byzantine painters. From the
top of the village of Loutsa, by following the signs (*right*)
for the restored church of Aghios Dimitrios, then right
again for 500m, you come to a small, cruciform church
beside a plane tree known as **Palaia Panaghia** (*for which
the key should be obtained beforehand from the Pappás in
Stení*). The windowless structure—now supported in a
concrete frame to keep it standing—probably dates from
the 12th century. The interior has extensive wall-paint-

ings of possibly a couple of centuries later, whose current condition impairs their legibility. To the north of Loutsa is the entrance to the majestic **Agali Gorge**, whose waters descend straight from the southern slopes of Dírfys, which rises 1500m unimpeded to the summit directly above.

Around Katheni

A short distance to the southwest of **Katheni** a sign points west down a track 2.5km to **Eriá** (or **Moni Erión**), which lies amongst trees beside the lower reaches of the Koumbes Torrent which descends originally from the Agali Gorge. The church is dedicated to the Presentation or Purification of the Virgin. Almost the entirety of its 13th century, cruciform plan, c. 4m x 4m, is surmounted by a disproportionately high dome. All the surfaces inside are painted, but much blackened with candle-soot. The surrounding monastery buildings were destroyed in 1840, and only the church, or *catholicon*, now remains. The springs here once fed the Ottoman aqueduct to Chalcis.

Around Voúni

A different design of ecclesiastical building, but one particular to Euboea, is encountered in the two beautiful 13th century churches at **Voúni** (5km southwest of Stení), both of which lie to the south side of the main village road: the churches of the **Metamorphosis** ('Transfiguration') and, further to the west, of the **Aghii Apostoli**. Both are of substantial size and built on a rectangular plan with an apse. The cruciform element of their design is intimated by the elevated, transverse vault which bisects them. This also gives both buildings their greater height. The church of the Metamorphosis has also had a later narthex added and possesses an independent belfry. This is an early example of a free-standing belfry and it may represent an interesting innovation of Western, Frankish influence into Orthodox architecture of the 13th century.

The Manikiotis Gorge and Makrichori

This area lies substantially further to the east, and is accessible by the scenic road which rises north from Amarynthos through a sea of olive-groves, into the eastern foot-hills of Mount Olympos, with wide, unfolding **views** across the island and the straits. The road levels off on reaching the attractive mountain villages of **Séta** (57.5km from Steni and 19km from Amarynthos) and **Káto Séta**. At **Makrichóri** (65.3km), the early 14th century cemetery-church of **Aghios Dimitrios** lies just below the level of the road in the centre of the village. Once again the design—with narthex added later—has the elevated transverse vault in the middle. The interior possesses a simple altar and stone floor; but it is decorated with **15th century paintings** of considerable quality, although darkened with soot. After the next village, Maníkia, the road begins to descend the impressive *****gorge of the Manikiotis River**. The valley is deep and tranquil, hemmed by vertical scarps that rise to 800m on its north side. Shortly before the gorge ends just to the west of the village of Koíli, some stretches of well-constructed **polygonal walling**, suggesting that the entrance was once marked by a fortified look-out in antiquity, are visible on the 'bastion' of cliff to the north of the road. (*These are high up on the precipice above the entrance to the gorge, just below the summit: they can best be seen from a point on the last level stretch of road, before the final descent by switchbacks.*) Further west of these, a mediaeval tower still stands on the crest. From the gorge the road drops into the lush, hilly country of the eastern corner of central Euboea, whose natural centre for exploration is Kymi.

KYMI & THE CENTRAL
EAST OF THE ISLAND

(*Kymi = 0.0km for distances in this section*)

In common with other towns which were founded or re-
founded in the 18th century and which knew a modest
prosperity during the 19th century, **Kymi** has a stately air
imparted to it by its gardened villas and streets of stone
houses. It is famous for its figs and honey, and grew rich
on a strong maritime tradition; in 1821 it put to sea a
fleet of 55 merchant ships, which earned it a bombard-
ment from the Turks. Much of the town is a loosely connected series of semi-rural neighbourhoods, stretching
over the hills and looking out to Skyros over the island's
Aegean coast. The spirit of the place is pleasingly captured in the **Kymi Folklore Museum** (*open daily 10–1,
5–7.30*) laid out in a late 19th century neoclassical town-
house, to the right of the road as you exit the centre for
the port.

The collection is comprehensive and well-displayed, with
exhibits from every aspect of local life. The embroideries,
textiles, lace-work and costumes are of great refinement
here. A number of maritime pictures are of interest and,

amongst the household and agricultural implements of the last century, are many that would not have been unfamiliar to the Ancients: shepherds' sandals and a plough—seemingly straight from Hesiod; wine-presses; ingenious fisherman's warning buoys with bells; soap- and wax-making apparatus; and a silk-worm incubator.

To the north of Kymi a road descends through a valley of plane-trees to the **springs** (1.5km) of the town's homonymous mineral water, which is now bottled and distributed all over Greece: the water is exceptionally soft and similar in flavour to that of Sariza on Andros.

The road which leaves the town to the east and then heads north, terminates at the immaculately kept **convent of the Transfiguration** (Metamorphosis tou Sotiros) (4km) founded in the 17th century on what has been tendentiously claimed to be the site of Ancient *Kyme*. The setting is panoramic (towards Skyros) and protected; it is well-endowed with water (generous springs at Gournia, 500m south), and possesses a natural acropolis above, now occupied by the remains of the Venetian **castle of Aghios Giorgios**.

Below Kymi to the east (3.5km) is the port which serves the ferry crossing to Skyros: the island is an administrative province of the nome of Euboea. From Platána on the coast to the south of the port, a road leads uphill to the west for 3km as far as the archaeological site at **Ano Potamiá** (9km) on the summit of a steep, conical hill. (*Access is easiest by the west slope; the east slope, which preserves substantial stretches of wall, is densely covered with oak and undergrowth.*) The ruins extend over a large area: at the crown of the hill is the well-preserved base of a **fortress of Hellenistic times**, including the remains of adjacent buildings—possibly barracks—and dwellings, one one of which possesses a baking oven. The area is scattered with potsherds, broken tiles, and fragments of white marble. The earliest habitation on the site goes back to Neolithic times (4th millennium BC), at which time the settlement was located in the saddle between this and the hill to the south. The small **museum** (*no fixed opening times: ask locally for the 'phylax'*) in a converted hall beside the church in the nearby village of Potamiá, contains the artefacts from the various periods which have been found at the site.

The debate as to whether the remains on this hill are those of the ancient town of *Oechalia*, mentioned by Pausanias (*Descrip*. IV.2.3), cannot be resolved on the basis of existing evidence. The debate also raises the question of the location of the city of Ancient *Kyme*—an important centre in antiquity, not least because it is said by Strabo to have been the co-founder (together with Chalcis) of its homonymous colony, *Cumae*, in the Bay of Naples in Italy. Some scholars thought that the true founder of the colony was a city of the same name in Aetolia: others have even doubted the very existence of a Euboean *Kyme*. Visible remains and archaeological finds, however, from the hill of Viglatouri at Oxylithos suggest that the site of the city which seeded *Cumae* in the 8th century BC may have been on its slopes. They bear witness to a continuous habitation from the Middle Helladic period (early 2nd millennium BC), through Mycenaean times and well into the Late Geometric era.

SIX BYZANTINE CHURCHES:
OXYLITHOS & AVLONARI

The wide, fertile valley that stretches to the south of Kymi as far as the lake of Dystos, knew considerable prosperity in the 13th and 14th centuries. As a consequence it is dotted with a great number of churches from this period, many of which have wall-paintings executed by a school of artists of widely varying skills. Six of the most important churches are described below. They are grouped around two principal centres: Oxýlithos and Avlonári.

Immediately noticeable from the coast road south beyond Platána is the sharp conical peak of an extinct volcano (now crowned by a modern church of little architectural merit but with wonderful views), around which the village of **Oxýlithos** (10km) is clustered. The road south out of the village makes a sharp bend around a modern church: down the hill which leads out of the curve of the bend is the tiny, 13th century chapel of **Aghia Anna** (1) decorated with **wall-paintings** executed in different periods. The fine Pantocrator in the ceiling is by a more sophisticated hand than the scenes on the south wall which are of later date. Close by and of greater architectural interest is the church of the *****Theotokos** (2) (*on the left side of the main road, 300m beyond the modern church*). The unusual design is articulated in several successive developments: the nucleus is a small 13th century, vaulted chapel of rectangular plan with a small, faceted apse. This core segment possesses the characteristic Euboean elevated transverse barrel-vault bisecting the space. In the subsequent century a square, cross-vaulted narthex was added to the west. Finally, in the last 50 years, a modern vestibule was added yet further west. The interior has **wall-paintings** of the 15th century which are interesting both for their quality and subject-matter: in the cross-vaults of the narthex are visible *Christ at the well* *with the Woman of Samaria* (north) and a very literal interpretation of the text, '*Pick up thy bed and walk*' (east). In the same narthex, a *Dormition of the Virgin* (north) faces *St John dictating the Revelation to Prochoros* (south), with *Abraham and Sarah with the three Angels* (west). The floor, with elements in a yellow stone, is also of considerable age.

The most important and remarkable church in the area, and one of the finest in Euboea, is the large, 13th century basilica of **Aghios Demetrios** (3) which lies further south at **Hánia** (19km), just to the west of Avlonári. It is a church with a splendid presence both inside and out: broad, stable, pleasingly articulated in a complex of geometric volumes, and decorated externally with refined brick- and stone-work. The building has several unusual elements, such as the pointed arches of its interior, which reveal a marked Western or Frankish influence resulting from the Latin occupation of the island: indeed this feature tends to suggest that the elevated transverse vault with pitched roof in lieu of a dome, which is encountered so frequently in churches on Euboea, may be influenced by the transept-crossing of contemporaneous Western Gothic structures. As a design, it certainly represents a significant deviation from the traditional Byzantine circle-on-square design. It must also have reduced the complexity—and therefore the cost—of constructing such buildings.

The dedication to Aghios Demetrios is possibly significant given the church's rural position at the heart of a low-lying fertile area of cultivation—a configuration typical in ancient times for sanctuaries to Demeter. Aghios Demetrios frequently supersedes Demeter in the 'christianisation' of pagan sanctuaries: he was a Roman soldier turned Christian, and is often seen in icons dispatching a fellow heathen Roman soldier, neatly symbolising the victory of Christianity over the pagan. This story was then given further weight by the erection of a church to the saint over any site where Demeter had once been worshipped.

The overall form of the church is interesting and represents a rapid organic growth stretching over no more than a century and a half. The original 13th century core of the building (to the east) possesses the transverse barrel-vault mentioned above. Of almost contemporary construction is the low aisle or *parecclesion* to the north side, which may even have been in origin an open ambulatory which was later closed in. The narthex, which in contrast to the core building is surmounted by a dome with an external octagonal drum, dates from probably from the end of the 14th century—the period in which the aisle to the south may also have been added.

The *exterior* has beautiful features at both the east and west ends: an apse in fine **cloisonné brick and stone work** with a tri-lobe window, and an attractive surround to the west door with further brick embellishments, which are echoed in the frame of the niche above and in the brickwork below the eaves of the cupola.

In the *interior*, the broad, spacious, domed narthex immediately surprises with its wide pointed arches. The vestiges of a *Pantocrator* can be seen in the crown of the dome. The *naos* is entered through a narrow, steeply arched doorway, with two antique columns and capitals to either side. Not a lot remains of the **wall-paintings**, except for a fine face of St George (centre north wall) and a graphic *Last Supper Table*, laid with delicacies, visible above the templon-screen to the south side: their style would date them to the mid-15th century. Two 17th century candlesticks in *cipollino* marble stand before a masonry templon-screen incorporating **carved marble reliefs** in the lower area. The whole interior gives a sense of dignified spaciousness.

At the opposite end of the spectrum from this imposing church is the hidden, rural chapel of **Aghia Thekla** (4), 2.5km to the northwest. (*Branch left 1km north of Hánia; after a further 1km, take the first left turn to the village of Aghia Thekla. Just before the modern church in the village,* *a narrow road leads 50m steeply down to the chapel by a stream.*) In its delightful setting of plane-trees, running water and chanting nightingales, the 13th century chapel looks more like a cottage from a tale by Hans Christian Andersen than a church. Again the design is a simple apsed rectangle with elevated, transverse barrel-vault. Two artists are at work in the **murals**: the artist of the *Presentation of the Virgin* in the northwest corner has a much less sophisticated style than the talented 14th century artist of the figures to the south of the apse, whose hagiographic faces are at times inspiring.

The principal centre of this area of the island—an open landscape of volcanic hills framed by the mountain massif of Dírfys to the west and by the sea to the east, and dotted with robust towers on the hill-tops—is the attractive village of **Avlonári** (20km). Its narrow streets of balconied houses wind up to the summit of a hill, crowned by one of Euboea's best preserved **Frankish towers**, erected in 1260 over ancient foundations on the site of what is believed to have been an ancient sanctuary of Apollo. In the vicinity of Avlonári are two further churches with paintings that are worthy of note. First, in the centre of the village of **Pyrgi**, 2km north of Avlonári, is the 14th century **church of the Metamorphosis** (5), with the transverse-vault design, and a modern addition to the west. There are small areas of painting in good condition: the *Archangel Michael* and the *Entry into Jerusalem* on the north wall, reveal a high quality of workmanship, which must be almost contemporary with the church's construction. Second, in an isolated site in the area of Achladerí, east of Dáphni, 6.5km southeast of Avlonári, the monastery church of **Aghios Ioannis Prodromos of Karies** ('**Moni Karión**') (6) stands amid the ruins of its former conventual buildings. There is a **spring** of excellent water with a fountain-head of Byzantine design. The plan of the church is more traditionally Byzantine, with the central dome supported on four monolithic columns with antique capitals. Other pieces of re-used ancient marble in the vicinity suggest the preceding presence of a pagan structure. The masonry of the three facetted apses is reminiscent of the church of the Taxiarch at Melida on Andros. The interior, with flagstone floor, is vividly painted with 15th century **murals** of high quality.

LEPOURA TO ALIVERI

The long valley which stretched from the south coast of the island at Aliveri Bay up as far as Kymi on the north coast, was good agricultural land and formed one of the principal areas of interest and wealth for the Frankish settlers of the 13th century. For this reason their fortified towers are such a common feature of the landscape in this area. The biggest, and one of the oldest, of these Frankish strongholds was the early 13th century '**Rizokastro**' (33.6km), clearly visible on a hill 2km to the south of the main road, approximately half-way between Lépoura (29km) and Alivéri (36.5km). The remains consist of a well-preserved enceinte of walls surrounding a pre-existing tower. The castle was later fiercely contended between the Turks and Greek Independence fighters in the summer of 1823. Four kilometres due north of it, in the hilly area of the interior, is a church dedicated to Aghios Demetrios, but generally known as the '***Kókkini Ekklesía***', or 'Red Church' because of the preponderance of red tiles in its masonry. (*Best reached by the right turn (north) signed 'Aghios Demetrios', 1km east of the municipal limit of Alivéri. The road leads through olive groves and a functioning lignite and stone quarry; after 2.4km, the church is to the left, hidden, on a low hill.*) The church exemplifies the 14th century delight in decorative tile patterns: a cross pattern at the east end and a half-moon over the door. An ancient offering-table with three shallow depressions and a fragment of an Ionic capital are incorporated in the west front, with other ancient elements included elsewhere. There are vestiges of murals in the apsidal conch.

The remains of a vaulted **Mycenaean tomb** can be seen, 3.2km northwest of Lépoura on the cross-country route to Gavalás, via Katakaloú.

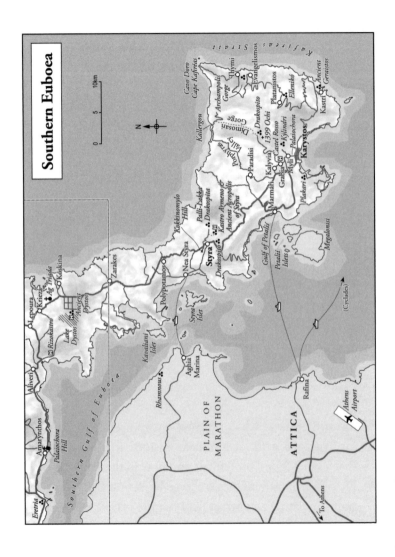

LAKE DYSTOS TO KARYSTOS, & AROUND MOUNT OCHI

(*Karystos = 0.0km for distances in this section*)

DYSTOS AND AGHIA TRIADA

Approached from any angle, the landscape of **Lake Dystos** (59km) is like a mirage: a strange cone of limestone rising from the middle of a sea of green, surrounded by bald hills. The alluvial lake itself, encircled by swallow-holes, is filled with water in spring and early summer, and then recedes to a verdant reed-bed in late summer and autumn. It shares a number of aspects of behaviour and appearance with Lake Copais across the water in neighbouring Boeotia, which is similarly a limestone-bound basin fed by seasonal waters. Lake Copais was the object of a massive project to drain and control its waters in prehistoric times which constitutes the earliest known, major hydraulic work of European history. It is interesting that a relief found on Euboea and now in the Museum of Epigraphy in Athens, bears a long 4th century BC inscription stipulating a contract between the people of *Eretria* (to which *Dystos* was subordinate) and an engineeer by the name of Chairephanis, to drain and control the water in Lake 'Ptechon' (namely, Dystos), using many of the means adopted centuries earlier at Copais. In recent years an attempt has been made to convert areas of the lake into arable land by filling.

The isolated hill on the lake's east side is the site of **Ancient *Dystos***, inhabited since the Neolithic period, and settled in earliest Antiquity by Dryopians—a Pelasgian, pre-Hellenic people of obscure origin. (*Access is by any of the tracks that lead west from the main road, south of the turn for Kóskina (58.5km). Dense vegetation has engulfed many of the remains still on the surface and makes explor-*

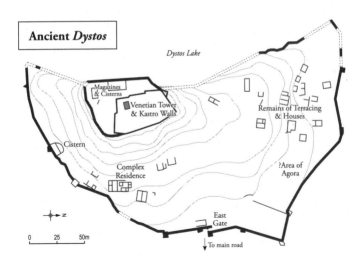

Ancient *Dystos*

Dystos Lake

Magazines & Cisterns

Venetian Tower & Kastro Walls

Remains of Terracing & Houses

Cistern

Complex Residence

?Area of Agora

East Gate

To main road

0   25   50m

*ing the site arduous. The walls and terraces alone stand
above the vegetation.*) The site is highly panoramic with
natural defences in the form of a steep drop to the lake on
the western side. Describing a wide semicircle eastward
from the west cliff, the line of the full enceinte of walls in
polygonal construction, dating from the late 5th century,
can be traced. The walls are 2m thick and in places still
stand to 3m in height. There were in all eleven towers, and
one gate with double bastions in the middle of the east
side, which led north into the area of the *agora*. On the
slopes of the hill—especially to the north where there are
also protrusions of terraces in a later, isodomic construction method—are the remains of a number of houses
built in ashlar masonry. They generally possessed an entrance passage, an inner court, a living room, bedrooms,
and in some cases an upper storey. At the summit of the
hill were the inner walls of the acropolis, the north part of
which was converted into a Venetian fortress and tower.

Some of the remains from *Dystos* made their way to the
curious, ruined mediaeval church of **Aghia Triada**, just to
the north. (*To the left, 1.2km south of Krieza, about 200m
before the descending road finally flattens out into the floor
of the Dystos valley.*) The lower areas of the apse and walls
still stand. The altar is a fluted column stump: the **central
door of the templon-screen**—an ancient sarcophagus,

standing on end, the bottom of which has been cut out, creating a single, stone, rectangular entrance-way—is an ingenious example of recycling.

STYRA

Between Lake Dystos and Styra, is a spring (54km: *4km south of the main Koskina junction*), whose water is locally much-prized, beside the road beneath the church of the Panaghia. At 50km the road passes **Zárakes**, 1km to the south of which are two ruined windmills which mark the site of some foundations, possibly of *Zaret(h)ra*, a place captured by the Athenian commander (and pupil of Plato), Phokion, in 350 BC. To the south of here, the windswept narrow ridges with views to the sea on both sides of the island have been dedicated to wind-farms which dominate the sky-line for a considerable distance.

(**Pálaia**) **Styra** (29km), a not unattractive village grouped around a *plateia* with trees, can make a good base for exploring the fascinating hinterland, whose vegetation is rapidly regenerating after the ravages of the catastrophic fires of 2007. On the west coast, 3.5km below, is the port of Néa Styra with a service by ferry approximately every two to three hours to Aghia Marina on the east coast of Attica. The site of Ancient *Styra*, still largely unexplored and unexcavated, lies inland of the shore; the ancient city's remarkable and remote acropolis, however, can be seen from many points on the road up to Palaio Styra—its megalithic portal silhouetted against the light, on the summit of the ridge over 600m above to the southeast. It is here that the most fascinating remains survive.

Styra is mentioned in the *Iliad* (Bk. II, 540) as participating in the Euboean expedition to Troy under the leadership of Elephenor. Although Herodotus sees its inhabitants as of Dryopian origin, Strabo relates that the city was settled by colonists from the Marathonian Tetrapolis (*Geog.* X, 6). In 490 BC it was taken by the Persian commander, Datis, and the offshore island of *Aigilia* was used for the safe-keeping of their hostages. *Styra* contributed two ships to the Greek force at Salamis in 480 BC and soldiers to the Battle of Plataea; as a consequence its name was engraved with those of other participating Greek cities on the serpentine bronze trophy, now in the Hippodrome in Istanbul. After 477 BC Styra was part of the Athenian Confederacy, and in 415 BC fought with Athens in the Sicilian campaign. In Roman times the acropolis area may have been used as a settlement for the quarry-workers employed in the exploitation of the local stone. The Venetians erected their fortress of Larmena or 'Armena', remains of which are visible today, on the site of the ancient fortifications.

The archaeological area (unsigned) of the quarries, the acropolis and the remarkable 'drakospita' or 'dragon's houses' (see pp. 117–118), are reached by taking the main road north from the square of (Palaia) Styra. After 800m, on a bend, take the asphalt road to the right; after a further 800m turn left onto a track, and then after 100m turn right. This track climbs for 1.5km, at which point it is necessary to turn right at what is the first opportunity. After 500m, fork left. After a further 500m the track splits: from this point, **left** *takes you, after 400m, to the foot of the hill where the* **drakospita** *(A) (10 mins) can be visited;* **right** *leads on up to the principal* **quarries** *(B) (20 mins) and the* **acropolis** *(C) (1 hr).*

Site A: The ('Palli-Lakka' group of) *Drakospita

This group of buildings is found after a short climb up from where the left-hand track ends, in a dip in the hillside facing west with a partial view down to the coast at Nea Styra and with relatively good visibility of the surrounding quarry area. As you approach you encounter:

• two parallel, rectangular buildings with impressive, pitched and corbelled roofs constructed from large schists, which at first sight have the appearance either of communal dwellings or large animal pens. A shallow-cut, stone basin sits by the corner of the nearest building;

- above and behind is a square building with a concentric, corbelled roof with an open 'oculus' in the centre, which would perhaps have been covered, if necessary, with ephemeral material. There is a stone corner-shelf inside;
- as you climb higher, you pass two rectangular basins cut in the rock: the one to the left has a small circular depression carved on its front;
- further up again is an elliptical stone construction built up against the wall of natural rock behind, with two small '*loculi*' to north and south, and a wall and doorway in front;
- substantially higher up, after crossing a scree of stones, is a vertical rock face (clearly cut by hand as evidenced by the chisel striations all over its surface) fenced by a wall and doorway in front. This would appear to be one of many quarry faces in the area. The rock face has a fissure (bottom right) facetted by human hand. On the right-hand wall, in front and inside of the entrance of the fissure, at a height of about 2m are a series of diagonal cuts in the rock—perhaps indicating approximate measurements for the quarrying.

The likely purpose

There have been wild surmises as to the date and epoch of these constructions—some commentators even extravagantly claiming them to be prehistoric places of cult. It should, however, be recalled that this whole area was dedicated in Antiquity to quarrying stone; that stone-working was the main economic activity of Karystos and Styra; and that a community of people therefore lived on site in these quarries, to avoid the laborious trek to and from the town each day. The mountains furthermore are subject to sudden storms and descending clouds for much of the early part of the year, and solid refuges would have been a real boon to the working community during the nights, and sometimes even during the day. The limestone quarried here naturally splits into large slabs or schists, and if you were going to build a structure in this area, the method of superimposing large slabs and corbelling them for the roof, constitutes in fact the easiest solution. The regular forms of the constructions and the roughly isodomic method (seen in much greater perfection in the *drakospito* at the summit of Mount Ochi), suggest that they emerge from a Hellenistic architectural background. They may well have been used in more recent times for penning animals for whom the water-basins would certainly have been useful. None of the above completely precludes that there was a cultic aspect to the buildings, beyond their purpose for refuge and storage; we know little about the people—who may have been immigrants from Caria—who worked in the quarries. Hercules (the archetypal 'labourer') was a popular divinity with stone-workers; but no archaeological evidence suggesting a cult of Hercules or any other divinity has been found yet at this particular site. It would in short be contentious to suggest any date prior to the 4th or 3rd centuries BC for these structures.

Site B: The main quarry area

The track and path up to the acropolis of Styra passes through the centre of the main, ancient limestone quarry—a series of small, quite deep, assays. As you climb (15 minutes) there are channels in the stone and terraces cleared in the rock. A number of shaped architectural pieces are still *in situ*: a finely **tapered column** (note the ring of circular indentations around the 'collar' for transportation); an abacus; several blocks of architrave with precise indentations. The rough-hewn '*dromos*', the long horizontal cuts and **cart-ruts** are evidence of the laborious task of transportation. Other ancient surface-quarries and screes of stone-refuse can be seen on the hillsides opposite.

Site C: The acropolis

The acropolis (reached after a 50-minute climb) is entered through the magnificent ***portal**, which is visible even from Nea Styra far below and commands views of the whole of the gulf of Euboea. It is composed of large monoliths of veined limestone, and its lintel is still in place. To the left, as you face the gate from outside, are vestiges of the ancient enceinte, dating probably from the 5th century BC or earlier. This site is an example of a natural rock acropolis which has been minimally modified and articulated to serve human ends. It is composed of a ridge of limestone 'tors', running northeast/southwest: the southwest tor has steps carved in its lower north side, which provided access to the look-out post on its summit. As you skirt the east side of the ridge towards the northeast tor, there are deep-cut post-holes in the rock and other cuts for gate posts at the northern extremity of the ancient, inner acropolis. Further north, you come to the tiny chapel of St Nicholas (with a rock-cut cistern in front of its west end), and the remains of the 15th century Venetian stronghold, the **Kastro Armeno**, now much dilapidated, which had two discrete entities: a main, impregnable 'keep' on the summit of the middle tor and fortifications with bastions on the northeastern summit. The *****view** takes in the sea to east and west, the three peaks of Attica in front, the Sounion peninsula, the islands of Makronisos, Kea and Skyros, the Boeotian coast, the Euripus, and Mounts Ochi, Dírfys and Kandili—in short, everything.

There are few other examples in the Greek world of an acropolis set so distantly from the city it served to protect: communications between the two that were not signalled must have taken a couple of hours. It is maybe more appropriate to see this as an almost independent, fortified look-out post and refuge settlement.

DRAKOSPITA

These remarkable, and often beautiful, megalithic constructions are unique to Euboea—which in itself is an odd fact. There are over 20 of them which have been identified on the island, mostly in the areas of Mount Ochi and of Styra. They are characterised by their construction method which employs massive, relatively flat stone slabs, meticulously corbelled roofs, and monolithic door posts and lintels. Most are rectangular: some have windows and indented niches or shelves inside. They are mostly solitary, and intentionally panoramic; but at Palli-Lakka below the acropolis on Styra, by contrast, they exist in a small group and in a more hidden position with limited visibility.

Their rarity and the remoteness of their sites have invited much speculation about both their date and purpose—ranging from those who wish to see them as prehistoric temples, to those who simply see them as sturdy animal pens. Buildings—as Ruskin observed—don't tell lies, as writers often are prone to do. The architectural milieu from which these buildings emerge is undoubtedly the world of late Classical and Hellenistic constructional practice: it is sufficient to compare design and masonry—especially of the *drakospito* on the summit of Mount Ochi—with, say, the Hellenistic fortified complex of Aghia Triada on Amorgos, to see that they belong to the same 'family' and epoch. The corbelling of the roof is a result of the properties of the natural stone in the area where they are found: it easily splits into large flat schists, making a corbelled roof the most logical and easiest solution for covering an open space. The majority of the *drakospita* are in the vicinity of stone-quarries on mountain sides, where refuges were necessary for the workers who lived among the quarries. Those that are not found near quarries, would appear to have served for surveillance. Most of the artefacts found at the same sites confirm a 4th–3rd century BC date. While it is true that objects of the 6th century BC and earlier have also been found at these sites, this does not necessarily indicate a date for the constructions, but only good evidence that their site was also frequented before the buildings were erected.

An interesting similarity has been noted between the *drakospita* and certain stone constructions in Asia Minor—namely dwellings said to have been built by the Lelegians, probably in the late 5th century BC in a distinctive masonry which employs corbelled vaults, in the area of Syangela (Alâzeytin) and Theangela (Etrim), near Halicarnassus/Bodrum in Turkey. 'Lelegians' are a people hard to define: they are generally considered to be pre-Greek predecessors of the Carians. They have left no inscriptions, and appear to have been considered a culturally inferior people to the Carians, whose servants they were. Strabo (*Geog.* XIII, 1.59) says that they served the Carians as soldiers and became 'scattered throughout the whole of Greece, so that the tribe disappeared'. It is not impossible that some of them ended up on Euboea as quarry-workers, once again doing the heavy labour of social inferiors, and putting up constructions here in the only way they knew how.

KOKKINOMYLO HILL

Almost opposite the first turning towards the sites described above (800m north from the square of Styra), a
road to the *left* leads less than a kilometre northwest to the
hill of Kokkinomylo, where a small marble monument
enshrines the bones of **Elias Mavromichalis** (b. 1795)
who died on this spot in January 1822. Mavromichalis,
who hailed from a famous clan of patriots from the Mani
in the Peloponnese, was a redoubtable fighter for Greek
Independence. He had arrived in Euboea in early January
to give support to the island's resistance movement and
died a matter of days later. He made his last stand against
the Turks here in a windmill on this hill, remains of which
can still be seen, and died for his cause together with a
group of fellow revolutionaries.

KAPSALA

Between Styra and Kápsala, 1.5km to its south along the
main road, there are several **watermills** on the hillside
above the road. The road climbs steeply: 2.5km from Styra, in the crook of a sharp, left-hand, hairpin bend is another well-preserved **drakospito**, consisting of two chambers, one of which has its closed, corbelled roof intact,

and two corner shelves inside. The construction method is easily distinguished from that of the small-stone, rough walling nearby, which is of much later date.

MARMARI

From the watershed above Styra, the main road descends with wide views of the **gulf of Petalií** and its scattered islets, through an area still extensively quarried—this time not for the hard grey limestone which is extracted at Styra, but for a softer, crystalline, more translucent, veined marble, known since the Renaissance as '*cipollino*', which enjoyed immense popularity in Rome throughout the last four centuries of its history. The cutting of the road itself reveals the marble—albeit dusty and opaque—mostly grey and white in undulating veins, sometimes blue-grey, and sometimes (the type most prized by the Romans) in a beautiful sea-green and white. It is found in varying quality over the whole area which stretches from here through Marmári to Kárystos and beyond (*see box below*). **Marmári** (12km) takes its name from the commerce in this marble. Strabo mentions a temple to Apollo *Marmarinos* nearby. Today Marmári is a quiet resort, served by the most convenient crossing between the south of the island and the Attic mainland near to Athens: services run to Rafina, typically every three hours, four times daily, with increased frequency at the weekends.

MARMOR CARYSTIUM: 'CIPOLLINO' MARBLE

Of all the decorative marbles that the Romans extracted from the length and breadth of their Empire—from Aquitaine to the Egyptian Desert, from African Numidia to the Propontis—none had such apparent popularity or was so widely employed throughout the Empire as *marmor Carystium*, which was available in such inexhaustible quantities in the foothills of Mount Ochi, and emerged from nature in a never-ending variety of subtly different patterns. Elegant and cool in its delicate marine colour, with long, green-blue veins on a translucent background, it was never dull and yet never overly demanded attention. It enhanced any other marble combined with it, and above all set off the white marble of sculpture with exemplary elegance. It was abundant, resilient, adaptable to construction, and not difficult to work. The Renaissance stone-workers called it *Cipollino* ('onion-like') not so much because it has the appearance of sliced onion, but because the veins of mica which colour the calcareous body of the stone, cause it to be easily cut along the seams in the fashion of an onion.

Its illustrious career in Rome began, according to Cornelius Nepos (cited by Pliny, *Nat. Hist.* XXXVI 48) when it was introduced by Mamurra of Formiae, Julius Ceasar's chief engineer in Gaul. It was extensively used in the Roman and Imperial Fora (Basilica Aemilia, Temple of Vespasian, the House of the Vestal Virgins, the Palace of Domitian, Forum of Trajan, Basilica of Maxentius etc.), its translucence and colour being preserved and refreshed by annual applications of a solution of chalk and milk. Amongst the largest monolithic columns of Carystian marble are those supporting the portico of the Temple of Antoninus and Faustina overlooking the Forum: they measure 40 Roman feet (11.9m) and rise to 48 Rf (14.2m) with their Corinthian capitals. Interestingly, their girth and length is the same as those which have, for some reason, been left unfinished in the quarry at 'Kylindri' on Mount Ochi. This may have been a standard measure of column shaft however—albeit one rarely commissioned, because of the size and the problems inherent in its transportation. Lowering such massive weights down the mountainside in a controlled fashion and with minimum damage was a job of considerable complexity; at the port they were shipped to Rome, or other destinations, slung, just below water-level, between two barges lashed together in the form of a catamaran. Although this provided the best hope of stability at sea, many never made it to their destination.

The Romans also extracted asbestos (whose curious properties so fascinated them: see Strabo, *Geog.* X, 1.6) from these same hills. All this meant a wealth of commerce for the port of *Carystus*. The official who oversaw it all was a figure of some importance, as is suggested by the lavish funerary monument of the local quarry master, whose ruins are still visible in the city centre.

Cipollino is rarely seen properly polished today (apart from some statue-pedestals in the Vatican and Capitoline Museums in Rome), and it appears dull when not regularly maintained. Pieces can be gathered easily in the area of the quarries and are of a rewarding lustre and elegance when polished even by modern machinery.

From Marmári a road leads into the interior of the island, to the attractive village of **Paradísi** (12.5km) which has many stone houses in local vernacular architecture and pleasantly shaded tavernas. The road continues below the western slopes of Mount Ochi, past Aghios Dimitrios (where there is also a good taverna), and down the deep **Poprhyras Valley**, emerging onto the steep Aegean coast at Kallérgou.

KARYSTOS

The grand sweep of the setting of **Kárystos** is unexpected: the curve of its sheltered gulf, the majestic, concave rise of Mount Ochi behind and the openness of the amphitheatre formed by the mountain, have something of the magnificence of the south coast of Crete near Sfakiá, or even of the landscapes of eastern Anatolia. The site of Ancient *Karystos* lies a little to the north of the modern town, which was only created in the wake of the Greek Independence revolution; its acropolis is still prominently marked by the pinnacle of *Castel Rosso*, the rambling fortress, visible from all around, from which the Venetians held the south of the island.

Karystos is first mentioned in Book II of the *Iliad*: it took part in the Trojan War under the command of its king, Nauplios. In Classical times it became the principal commercial and cultural centre of Southern Euboea, issuing its own coinage in the 6th century BC. Glaukos, a boxer who was victor in the Olympic Games in 520 BC was from *Karystos*. Remembering is destruction in 490 BC at the hands of the Persians, the city allied with Xerxes in the second Persian invasion, and was later treated punitively for its 'Medising' by Themistocles as a result. It was part of the First and Second Athenian Confederacies, and after 338 BC came under Macedonian control. Apollodorus, a Comic dramatist, and Antigonus, a bronze sculptor and writer, were 3rd century BC natives of *Karystos*. The Romans took the city in 198 BC; their later exploitation of the marble quarries here made the city into an important and prosperous provincial centre—though Dio Chrysostom paints a (perhaps overly-rhetorical) picture of its economic decline already as early as the turn of the 2nd century AD.

The modern town is spacious and pleasant, but with an indefinable air of listlessness. Perhaps for this reason it is a peaceful place to choose as a base for exploring the south of the island. After the liberation of the city from the Turks in 1833, the centre was laid out on a grid pattern by the Bavarian architect, Bierbach, at the request of King

Otho who desired that the city be named 'Othonoupolis' in his honour. The focus was to be the square where the church of Aghios Nikolaos (1912) now stands. The plan languished: the neoclassical town hall on the north side was only completed at the beginning of the 20th century by private subscription.

One block north of the harbour (*intersection of Kótsika and Sahtoúri Streets*) are the remains of a 2nd century AD **Roman funerary monument** of an obviously wealthy official in charge of the marble quarries. It had the appearance of a small Ionic, peripteral temple, with 6 x 7 columns, and an entrance on the east side: its base and the cella threshold are visible. Some of the marble from the structure and one of its decorative elements—a carved **'tondo' depicting the bust of a man with a bridled horse** by his shoulder, which surmounted the doorway—is now incorporated, along with other antique marbles, in the east side of the 13th century tower on the harbour esplanade (east of Aiolou Street), known as the '**Bourtzi**'. The tower is a fortress, of irregular hexagonal form, with two cannon embrasures on the seaward wall, and well-preserved machicolations high up on the south wall.

Opposite is the city's small **Archaeological Museum** (*open daily 8.30–3, except Mon*), set back behind a small garden area scattered with various ancient columns—as well as a venerable, antique steam-roller made by Marshall & Sons of Gainsborough, and John Allen & Sons of Cowley, England. The collection is small, with clear didactic material, and several interesting inscriptions.

Room 1 displays the **finds from the *Drakospito*** on the summit of Mount Ochi—mostly pottery from the 4th and 3rd centuries BC, but also an early Archaic, bronze earring and other pieces showing earlier use of the site; finds from Neolithic through to Byzantine times from Plakari, to the west of Karystos; interesting evidence from a metallurgy workshop at Archampolis (east coast); (*nos 10 & 11*) **Megarian bowls** of the 3rd century BC with beautiful relief designs.

Room 2: a wide variety of calligraphy, from the 4th century BC to Byzantine times, is represented by the **inscriptions** displayed: one is a record of Karystian public debt to the citizens of *Histiaia* and *Thebes*, some words from which have been erased; another records a decreed request for a judicial arbitrator from Kimolos. There are fine Ionic capitals from *Geraistos* and *Karystos* (Palaiochora), a good selection of carved *stelai*, and a statue base with depictions of athletes and hunting scenes.

West of Karystos, at a distance of 2.5km is the coastal hill site of **Plakari**—important archaeologically, but with little to see for the general visitor. This was the site of the earliest settlement in the area (Late Neolithic), although there is ample evidence of later habitation too. The main centre for the area, however, moved to Karystos (the area known as Palaiochora, 2km to the north of the modern town)—probably in the aftermath of the Persian destruction of 490 BC, although the date of the transfer is still debated. Many of the finds from this site are exhibited in the Museum in Karystos.

NORTH OF KARYSTOS

In the valleys to the north of Karystos are several important sites and monuments.

- **Kalývia, Grabiá and Aghia Triada**
  At the top of the village of Kalývia, 3.5km north of Karystos is the attractive, late mediaeval **church of the Taxiarches**. The luminous interior incorporates some antique elements: the steep drum of the dome sits on four monolithic columns, each surmounted by a double capital—Byzantine, on top of Ionic. The whitewash has been removed to reveal a painting of

the *Pantocrator* over the apse. Due north of Karystos is Grabiá, where there are mineral springs of considerable force at the church of **Aghia Triada**, on the east side of the hill. Finds going back as far as Palaeolithic times have been made in the cave (*closed*) above the church, from one of the earliest human settlements on Euboea. In the depths of the cave is a watercourse with falls and pools.

• **Castel Rosso—the 'Red Castle'**
The site of the **Castel Rosso** (2.5km—*accessible either from Grabiá or from Mýli*), dominating the plain and bay of Karystos, has impressive natural defences to the north and east. It constituted the acropolis of Ancient *Karystos*, and the lower courses of the existing facetted west tower are composed of large, rectangular, poros blocks and courses of polished marble taken from ancient buildings and fortifications. The castle—which is the largest on the island—was built in the first decades of the 13th century by Ravano dalle Carceri, the triarch who had been awarded the southern third of Euboea by the Frankish overlord, Boniface of Monferrat (*see 'History', p.16*). In 1261, the Latin Emperor, Baldwin II, took refuge here when he was driven out of Byzantium. The castle was ef-

fectively under Venetian control from 1365 until the Turkish conquest of 1470. Why it became called 'Castel Rosso', when it is made of yellow and grey stone, is not clear.

Behind the castle to the northeast, the **mediaeval aqueduct** brought water from the springs on the hillside opposite. The conduit would always have been vulnerable to attack; there are cistern complexes, therefore, in the north corner of the enceinte, and a well, in addition, beneath the floor of the chapel of Prophitis Elias at the summit (*lift metal trap-door*). The impressive **gateway** and the five-sided eastern bastion have been to some degree rebuilt, and the square tower in the southwest corner, with artillery embrasures, is an Ottoman addition. Across the expanse of the bailey is an immense quantity of collapsed rubble, indicating that the interior of the enceinte was densely constructed with an eye to withstanding long sieges.

· **Mýli and Kýlindri**
The road north from Karystos, past the hospital, leads into the area of **Palaiochóra**, the site of Ancient *Karystos*, at the foot of the acropolis hill now crowned by the castle. It continues beyond, into the densely treed

valley of **Mýli** (3.5km), named from the water-mills which profit from its abundant water. The village is a welcome retreat in summer heat, with a couple of shaded tavernas. At the top of the village are vigorous **springs** of a good, but not particularly sweet, water. The road ends at the church of Aghii Theodori, where a path continues up the slopes of Mount Ochi to the ancient quarry at 'Kýlindri' and eventually to the summit of the mountain. (*From the end of the cement road, go straight and cross the stream bed. Ahead, you can see a first quarry to the right side of the gorge and the stream, then a second face much higher up; on top of this, you can make out the supine, abandoned columns. This is the objective: it is 40 minutes uphill to your right (northeast), about 300m higher than the point of departure.*)

   *Kýlindri is a truly remarkable and evocative site. The half-dozen abandoned monolithic columns, some detached from the rock bed, others at a still more protean stage, are of massive dimensions: approximately 12m (40 Roman feet) in length, with a diameter of 1.26m (4.25 Roman feet): they already have a gentle, swelling entasis and cuffs at either end. They await a shipment that never materialised. The square holes in the bed-rock are for the fixing of pegs

and capstans for lifting and manoeuvering the columns. From this vantage point the port of Karystos, where the monoliths would have been loaded onto boats, looks despairingly far away over a terrain that presents seemingly insurmountable problems to the transportation of such cumbersome weights. Yet, by the construction of pistes of beaten earth, the use of braked sleds, and of calibrated rolling at other moments, such blocks were moved in large numbers down to the port, and then shipped, slung between two lashed barges, to their destination. All around are other quarries, cutting-faces and assays: it was the quarry-master's expertise that selected the best veins. Below, as you descend, you see a flat-topped rectangular knob which remains from the surface quarrying of thin decorative plaques of marble, cut from the bedrock.

•   **Mount Ochi**

There are several routes up to the **summit** of Mount Ochi (1,399m): it can be reached with some difficulty in 3 hours from Kylindri. The easiest and safest route is from the northwest, where the mountain road which continues high above Grabiá eventually brings you to a little over 900m a.s.l., from where the peak is

visible and can be reached with a further climb of little over an hour. The path, latterly very steep, is hinted
by stone cairns. Cloud can suddenly and unpredict-
ably envelop the summit, and care should be taken
to ensure that weather conditions and pressure are
stable before attempting the climb.

The summit is a line of eroded tors, more reminiscent of sculpture than a mountain peak. It is marked
by the chapel of Prophitis Elias. Fifty metres further
east, right on the ridge, is the *drakóspito*—the finest
of all *drakospita*, and one of the most extraordinary
and unexpected sights in Greece. It camouflages itself
so well against a background of the rock from which
it is made, that it can be missed at first. Symmetrical,
pleasingly proportioned, and precisely constructed
in horizontal courses of blocks with often beautifully
drafted borders, it could not be anything other than a
Hellenistic construction. The posts and lintels of the
doorway, and the adjacent blocks, are magnificent:
and the long interior space is beautifully corbelled.
There are windows (unusually) and niches in the
double south wall: the aperture of the door faces 15°
off due south. All around are pieces of stone with per-
forations or shapes that have been worked by hand.

If the building were simply a refuge for quarry-workers, it is hard to explain why it was built at the summit of the mountain—an area very difficult of access and considerably beyond the practical altitude for quarrying. No archaeological or constructional evidence suggests any cultic use on the site. So the most likely explanation is that the building served as the look-out post for a small garrison. For military surveillance, the views in all directions and over the commercially crucial straits between Euboea and Andros could not be better. The crucial question remaining is how the information relating to what was observed from this altitude was quickly and effectively communicated to the cities of *Geraistos* and *Karystos* below. Very frequently nothing at all can be seen from this point except the inside of a cloud.

EAST OF KARYSTOS

The southeastern seaboard of Euboea, was one of the most vital maritime traffic corridors in the ancient Aegean, on the route between the Black Sea and the commercial centres of mainland Greece—Athens and Corinth. It was also well-known for being one of the windiest and most tempestuous channels in the Aegean, funnelling the wind just as effectively as it funnelled the commercial traffic. This coastline is what Herodotus was referring to as the 'the hollows' (τὰ κοῖλα) in Book VIII. 13 of his *Histories*, when recounting how an entire Persian squadron came to grief on the rocks here in a storm in 480 BC. The ancient city of **Geraistos**, at the southern end of this coast, profited richly from the tariffs it levied on the wealth of passing commercial traffic. Its site, which corresponds to the protected bay of **Kastrí** (18km), is hard to reach today (*take the unmade track descending from the asphalted road just after it turns sharply north, 11km from Karystos*). By the bay—in a field to the right, c. 400m before the track ends at the church of the Zöodochos Pigi—are the vestiges of a classical temple. Large architectural blocks, one with a clearly conserved triglyph, mark the site of what may have been a temple of Poseidon: other material from the site has been taken to the museum in Karystos. It is now a wild and inaccessible place; but to the ancient seaman it was a welcome and busy haven in bad weather.

The long coastal valleys in this area which push deep inland, one after another, have the remote feel of a frontier land: the villages are exiguous, but the land is in parts fertile and watered by streams that flow down from the heights of Mount Ochi, dense with oleander and plane-trees. One of the villages, **Platanistós**, takes its name from these trees. One kilometre after leaving the settlement of

Platanistos, a track leads down steeply into the valley to the right (*signed to 'Anemopilies' and 'Aghios Konstantinos'*). After 1.2km you reach the site of **Ellenikó**, which dates probably from the mid 5th century BC. In the middle of the steep fields the corner of some massive stone terracing rises from the vegetation, constructed in horizontal courses of masonry of varying width. The church of Aghios Konstantinos, further to the west, incorporates ancient blocks and elements in its walls. An inscription from here mentioning Artemis *Bolosia* is all that we have to help identify the site.

Twenty kilometres beyond Platanistos the unsurfaced road turns west and begins to circumvent the **Archampolis Gorge**. This wild and majestic landscape appears to have been inhabited in Antiquity and, although no city or town as such has been identified, the scattered remains which have been found may well have belonged to a single, organised, but scattered, settlement. Habitation seems to stretch from the Archaic period through to the 1st century BC, when the area was abandoned, perhaps following an attack by Mithridates in 80 BC. An acropolis (on the conical eminence overlooking the outlet to the sea), a large *drakospito*-like structure with evidence—unusually—both of residential *and* possible cultic use, a farmstead, and an iron-ore smelting furnace and workshop have all been located within a circumscribed area, near the riverbed at the eastern end of the valley. (*The sites are best reached by the footpath which leads from the road just to the north of the settlement of Evangelismos—which lies to the south of the gorge—and descends north into the valley. A similar but longer foot-path descends south from the houses at Thymi, which lies to the north of the gorge.*)

The road, now mostly un-surfaced, continues north as far as **Cape Kafiréas**—known also by its Venetian name of 'Cavo Doro'—where Nauplios, father of Palamedes, is said to have lighted torches to mislead the Greeks on their return from Troy, in revenge for the murder of his son on a false charge of treachery. The scattered villages of this area are still inhabited by the descendants of the Albanians who were settled here by the Venetians in the 15th century.

Time and patience, and strong legs or a strong vehicle are needed to explore further in this area: there are no road-signs and because the roads on the ground often do not correspond to those on the older maps, a detailed and up-to-date map of the area is essential. Those who have the energy to explore, however, will be rewarded—especially on the north side of the mountain—by some grand and beautiful valleys, rich in flora, butterflies and fauna. Mediaeval mule-paths and stone *kalderimi* can be followed along the scenic **Dimosari Gorge**, for example. From the same point, mentioned above (*see p. 133*) for commencing the climb to the summit of Ochi, a path to the north leads down into the gorge. At least eight hours should be allowed for the journey down to the shore and back. There is fresh water running in falls, almost all the way down to the sea.

PRACTICAL INFORMATION

340 01-346 00 **Evia**, **Evvia** or **Evvoia**: area 3,661 sq.km; perimeter 729km; resident population 191,009; max. altitude 1743 m. **Port Authorities**: Agiokampos T. 22260 71228; Aedipsos T. 22260 22464; Chalcis T. 22210 22236; Eretria T. 22290 62201; Kymi T. 22220 22606; Nea Styra T. 22240 41266; Marmari T. 22240 31222. **Information**: T. 22210 82677, www.naevias.gr

ACCESS

Access to the island is either by road via the Euripus bridges (1 hr from Athens, exit 'Schimatari' from Athens/Thessaloniki autoroute) or via short ferry crossings from Rafina (Attica) to Marmaris (c. every 3 hrs), Aghia Marina (Attica) to Nea Styra (c. every 2–3 hrs), Skala Oropou (Atti ca) to Eretria (every 30 mins), Arkitsa (Phthiotis) to Aedipsos (hourly), Glyfa (Phthiotis) to Agiokampos (hourly). A hydrofoil service, four times weekly in the summer also links Chalcis with Limni, and Limni with Loutrá Aedipsoú and Aghios Konstantinos.

LODGING

North Euboea. Spa hotels in Aedipsos: the luxurious **Thermae Sylla Spa** (*T. 22260 60100, fax 22055, www.thermaesylla.gr*) or the **Avra Spa Hotel** (*T. 22260 22226, fax 23260*). Alternatively, the **Hotel Aigli** (*T. 22260 22215, fax 24886*), is a comfortable hotel, without spa facilities. In Limni, choice is limited: the **Hotel Plaza** (*T. 22270 31235, fax 31336*), on the water front is quiet and simple, and currently represents the best option.

Central Euboea. At Steni, the **Hotel Dirphys** (*T. 22280 51217*) is tranquil and delightful, but very basic. Chalcis is not an obvious choice to stay in but if necessary, the **Paliria Hotel** (*T. 22210 28001, fax*

81959), near the museum is a pleasant option. At Kymi the **Hotel Corali** (*T. 22220 22212, fax 22002, www.coralihotel. gr*), a little way outside the harbour, is modern and comfortable.

Southern Euboea. At Karystos the **Apollon Suites Hotel** (*T. 22240 22045, fax 22049 www.apollonsuiteshotel.com*) is an Italian-run hotel on the beach, with large rooms, to the eastern end of the town. Closer in to the centre is the **Hotel Karystion** (*T. 22240 22391, fax 22727, www.karystion.gr*) less spacious, but a little more modern and stylish, and with pleasant service.

Historic Villa Rentals

For those seeking a luxurious base for a longer period (preferably in a small group so as to share the cost) these two historic houses are excellent and elegant solutions: **Villa Averoff** at Kirinthos, (*www.villa-averoff.com*); and the **Konaki** at Prokopi (*www.candili.gr*).

EATING

In Aedipsos, the central **Mezedopoleion Armenizontas** often has good, live *rebetiko* music. In Limni, **To Kyma** (new), in a handsome stone house on the waterfront, is attentive both to service and to the freshness of its delightful variety of classic, Greek dishes. The well-established **To Astro**, at Katounia, remains good for fresh fish. **To Neon**, 1km below Stení, delightfully spread out beneath immemorial planes by a stream, spe-

cialises in local sausage and charcoal grilled vegetables and meats. **Geroplatanos** in Myli, near Karystos, is somewhat similar in setting, with a good choice of dishes, especially at lunchtime on Sundays. In Karystos itself, Kotsika Street is lined with simple, inexpensive street-eateries; these may look uninspiring, but do not underestimate the quality of meat and the freshness of the wine at the minuscule **I Melissa**, at no 27

FURTHER READING

Sarah Wheeler, *An Island Apart,* 1992; Barbro Noel-Baker, *An Isle of Greece: The Noels in Euboea* (2000), Archaeopress, Oxford; or from www.deniseharveypublisher.gr

GLOSSARY

abacus—the (usually square) upper part of a column capital, directly below the architrave

aghiasma—a place where there is holy water; a holy spring

agora—a large public space, mainly given over to commerce

anthemion—a decoration with a flower- or palmette-based design, often placed on the pinnacle of a pediment

Archaic period—the 7th and 6th centuries BC

ashlar—stone masonry using large, dressed, regular blocks

Boeotia—the region and prefecture of central Greece which lies directly north of Attica and west of Euboea

catholicon—the church at the centre of an Orthodox monastery

cavea—the hemicycle of seats accommodating the public in a theatre

cella—the interior space of a temple (cp. *naos*)

clerurch—the settler of an imposed colony whose is able to keep the citizenship of the colonising city

cloisonné—(in masonry) the 'framing' or separating of cut blocks of stone with thin ceramic tiles in the construction of a wall

crepidoma—the platform of a temple in its entirety, often consisting of three superimposed levels which successively decrease in size

dromos—an entrance passage or axial approach to a tomb or building

entablature—the part of an ancient building above the columns (the architrave, frieze, cornice, etc.)

Geometric period—the 10th–late 8th centuries BC

Hellenistic period—era of, and after, the campaigns of Alexander the Great, c. 330–c. 150 BC

heroön—a monument or building (generally circular) which commemorates a hero or mythical person

himation—an ancient, rectangular (linen or woollen) garment worn around the body and draped over the left shoulder

hyposkenion—the rooms or space below the main stage in an ancient theatre

iconostasis—the high wooden screen (generally holding icons and images) which separates the sanctuary from the main body of an Orthodox church and which with time came to substitute the masonry *templon* (*see below*) of earlier Byzantine churches

isodomic—(of masonry) constructed in parallel courses of neatly-cut rectangular blocks

jamb—the side-post of a door- or window-frame

kalderimi—a stone-paved or cobbled pathway or mule-track

kouros—the statue of a nude, male figure, common in Archaic sculpture

loculi—compartments, or excavated rectangular tombs, for burial

machicolation—a defensive projection out from a fortified building, often over the entrance or at a corner, from which projectiles or hot liquids could be dropped on assailants

megaron—the great hall of a Mycenaean palace, rectangular in shape and generally preceded by a porch

naos—the central interior area of a Byzantine church or the inside chamber of a pagan temple

narthex—the entrance vestibule of a Byzantine church, often running the width of the building

nome (νομός)—a prefecture and administrative division of Greece

nymphs—divinities of springs, grottoes and pools of water

orchestra—the circular, or partially circular, floor of a theatre reserved for the chorus and for dance

parecclesion—a discrete chapel attached and parallel to a larger main church *peripteral*—of a temple which is surrounded by a peristyle of columns

Phthiotis—the prefecture of central Greece bordering the Malian gulf into which the northwestern part of Euboea projects

phylax—the custodian of a site or museum

pithos (pl. *pithoi*)—a large, tall, ceramic storage jar, sometimes used also for burials

protome—a carved projection in human or animal form (most frequently head only) on an object or building (similar in some ways to a 'gargoyle')

socle—a (slightly protruding) ledge forming the foundation of a wall

Sotir—(as a church dedication) the Saviour

spolia—elements and fragments from ancient buildings re-used in later constructions

stele (pl. *stelai*)—a carved tablet or grave-stone

templon—the stone or masonry screen in a church which closes off the sanctuary

tholos—a circular building, generally covered with a vault or cupola

thesmophoreion—a place for the ritual worship of Demeter, mostly frequented by women

volute—an architectural feature or support in the form of a spiral scrol

INDEX

Nigel McGilchrist is an art historian who has lived
in the Mediterranean—Italy, Greece and Turkey—
for over 30 years, working for a period for the
Italian Ministry of Arts and then for six years as
Director of the Anglo-Italian Institute in Rome.
He has taught at the University of Rome, for the
University of Massachusetts, and was for seven
years Dean of European Studies for a consortium of
American universities. He lectures widely in art and
archaeology at museums and institutions in Europe
and the United States, and lives near Orvieto.